Creative
Bible Study

Creative
Bible Study

A handbook for small group, family,
and personal Bible Study with
"Adventure" questions for discussion

by

LAWRENCE O. RICHARDS

ZONDERVAN PUBLISHING HOUSE
A DIVISION OF THE ZONDERVAN CORPORATION
GRAND RAPIDS, MICHIGAN

96548

CREATIVE BIBLE STUDY
© 1971 by Zondervan Publishing House,
Grand Rapids, Michigan

Second printing 1972

Library of Congress Catalog Card Number 78-156244

Unless otherwise indicated, the Scripture quotations in this book
are taken from *The New Testament in Modern English*
© 1958 by J. B. Phillips, and are used by permission
of the publisher, The Macmillan Company.

Printed in the United States of America

To my wife
MARTHA
*whose role in the writing of this book
and the shaping of my life
will become more clear
to all who read it.*

Contents

SECTION THREE: RESOURCES

Introduction

CREATIVE BIBLE STUDY?

For a long time we evangelicals have urged one another to study the Bible. And while we've nodded approval to such exhortations, we've failed dismally to do it. But today the renewal God is bringing to many believers and to their churches is focusing fresh interest on the study of God's Word. Particularly we see new concern for studying the Bible together — with others.

And so it's time to rethink our approach to Bible study; to discover how to explore God's living Word. It's time, in fact, to begin a lifetime of creative Bible study.

But before we begin afresh, it's helpful to ask about why we've failed to become involved, as a people, in God's Word. I believe there are three primary causes for our past failures. (1) We've carried to our study of Scripture hidden assumptions, or perspectives on life, that obscure what God is saying to us. (2) We've approached the Bible as though studying it were solely an individual exercise, and have failed to seek the sharing ministry of others in understanding and living it. (3) We have lacked the right tools, or methods of study, that would help us clarify the meaning and applicability of the text.

It's to meet these three problems that *Creative Bible Study* has been written. And perhaps to encourage us to fresh attempts to discover in God's transforming Word all He has promised us through it.

The Problem of Perspective

We all "see" and "hear" from a particular perspective; a viewpoint from which we interpret what others say and do. We can see the impact of perspective easily when we look across cultures. A missionary announces services for 9:30 Sunday morning in a Filipino village — and is greatly upset when the people straggle in a half hour to 45 minutes late. He feels this is an insult. But the people aren't really insulting him. They respect him, or they'd never show up so promptly. They would never show up at all!

What's the problem? One of perspective. The missionary, from a Western culture, looks at "time" and "being on time" in a completely different way than do the people to whom he is ministering. They have a different perspective. And until he learns to understand their viewpoint, he'll find it impossible to interpret accurately the meaning of what they do and say. Misunderstanding is inevitable.

The same problem operates in any interpersonal relationship. For years I thought that helping my wife with certain household chores was a clear demonstration of love. I was jolted when I discovered that she didn't see my actions as love-demonstrating at all. They seemed instead covert criticism of her housekeeping! Our perspectives, our hidden assumptions about the meaning of things we said and did, led to serious misunderstanding.

It is important to realize that perspective *always* colors our understanding of words and actions. And the greater the difference in perspective, the greater the potential for misunderstanding. When we come to the Book which records God's thoughts and actions and His words to us, there is bound to be misunderstanding until we clarify the perspective, the viewpoint, from which God's words are spoken.

Actually, we can't help reading the Bible from a human, cultural and personal viewpoint. Fallen man views life and relationships from a perspective that has been warped by sin. He does not "naturally" think about things God's way. To make it worse, all of us are bound, to some extent, by our culture. Our thought patterns, our ways of looking at life, always reflect the views current in our society. And finally, each of us has had personal experiences which color our viewpoints. Such a simple thing as the way our human fathers treated us can't help but color our perception of God when we think of Him as "Our Father in Heaven." *Unless we carefully examine the hidden assumptions that constitute our perspective, and seek to discover God's unique perspec-*

tive on issues critical to understanding Scripture, we are bound to misunderstand. And, misunderstanding, we will find the Bible a disappointing book.

Each chapter in section one of this book focuses on a critical issue of perspective, trying to clarify the unique perspective from which God speaks, so that we can learn to understand His words in His way — not in ours. * You'll find chapters introduced with a brief statement of the principle to be discussed in it. The chapters themselves are designed to help the reader feel as well as gain an intellectual grasp of the issue being considered. My conviction is that when we learn to read the Bible *from God's viewpoint,* and only then, can we discover that it is truly a Living Word.

The Problem of Isolation

I'm convinced that many of us have experienced difficulty in Bible study because we have thought of it as something to be done in private — alone, with no need for sharing with others. Part of the difficulty with this approach is that it thrusts the total responsibility for continuing our study on the individual — and as a people we are not noted for self-discipline. We need the support and encouragement that responsibility to others promotes — a phenomenon demonstrated in the success of the popular "weight watchers" program.

Even more serious, however, is the fact that God's Word in *meant* to be studied corporately. We see indications of this in Scriptural injunctions to come together for mutual encouragement and exhortation (Heb. 10:24, 25), and in descriptions of early church meetings (1 Cor. 14:26f). It is made more clear in the Bible's description of our interdependence — our need to give and to receive from other believers. Sharing together, centered in the Word of God, is an essential element in Christian growth. The Bible makes it clear that maturity in love comes through "that which every joint supplies" when each part is functioning — and the "joints" and "parts" are individual members of Christ's

---

* Seminarians will find that "hermeneutical principles" (e.g., basic principles for understanding and interpreting Scripture) are what I am dealing with here. That is, this is a book on Bible study that starts from a hermeneutical rather than a *methods* premise.

church who, together, form the Christian community (Eph. 4:16). Somehow, then, we need to come to the Word of God together, sharing our lives and submitting ourselves to God as He speaks to us.

We all have problems in coming together. We need help to develop the openness and honesty which permits us to expose ourselves to Scripture's searching gaze. We need this help just as much as we need to come to Scripture and read it from God's perspective, with all our hidden assumptions recognized and stripped away.

And so this book is designed to speak to the problem of isolation as well as the problem of perspective. How? Following each section you'll find a series of activities suggested for a group — either a family group, or eight or ten concerned Christians who want to share and grow together. These activities are designed to help you learn to share with each other, and thus move toward true community and interdependence. And at the same time the activities will help you think together about the principles developed in the chapters — and to study God's Word together from their perspective.

The Problem of Understanding

While the first section of this book concentrates on the subjective, "within us" factors that block Bible study, the second concentrates on objective factors. Perhaps I can put it this way. With other conservative evangelicals, I view the Bible as God's Word — His Truth revealed to us. The Bible thus contains objective, accurate information about God, about us, about His past working and His present purpose and His certain promise for the future. This information is vitally important to us, not only because it helps us understand our world and our God, but because it provides the basic understanding and interpretation of life that we need to live in harmony with God. The Bible shows us reality — and invites us to experience it.

Part two concentrates on that objective understanding and interpretation of life that *is there,* in Scripture, and helps you discover and accurately interpret the reality that is portrayed in God's Word.

The section is divided into two parts. The first, "Life at

Issue," shows how to start from personal experiences and concerns and approach Scripture to find guidance. The second, "Building Understanding," shows how to start with Scripture itself, and work from the objective interpretation of a book or passage to personal application.

A third section of the book gives information and ideas for going beyond the sessions outlined in this book, in a continuing experience of sharing God's Word together.

Using Creative Bible Study

Creative Bible Study is designed to speak to each of the three major blocks to meaningful Bible study outlined above. And to do it in a creative way; out of the pattern of most "methods" books and "how to" classes. It is designed to give specific guidance to those who want to *learn by doing*, and so to discover the excitement of exploring God's Living Word.

To be most effective, whether used in classroom or local congregation, the book should be used in a small group, action study context. That is, those who want to rediscover God's Word for themselves should be formed in small groups, and commit themselves to prepare for and participate in the twenty two-hour sessions needed to work through the book. While I hope the chapters will be helpful even to the casual reader, I have no doubt that those who take the group approach, opening themselves up to God and one another, will profit most. And will discover firsthand the creative power of Bible study.

LARRY RICHARDS
August, 1971

Creative
Bible Study

1
Not Just for Learning — Life!

"My!" Carole exclaimed admiringly.
"Jack surely knows a lot about the Bible."
We ought to admire people who know
a lot about the Bible — they demonstrate
a commitment to study and to Scripture
that's admirable. But somehow, just
"learning a lot about the Bible" doesn't
excite most of us. And that's good. It
shouldn't.
For studying the Bible isn't an end. It's
a means.

Some of my driest times spiritually came while I was in
seminary, studying the Bible every day. I know it's not
supposed to be that way. But it was, for me, and for lots
of others.

After all, there's nothing magical about the Bible. A
chapter a day doesn't keep the doldrums away. Hours in
and out of the classroom getting to know a lot about Scripture doesn't work like Alice's magic mushroom, and transform one into a spiritual giant. Knowing a lot about Scripture — knowing God's point of view, and getting to see things
His way — *is* important for every Christian. Of course. But
not as an end in itself. Getting into the Bible is important
as a means; a means God uses to bring our life and thought
and action into harmony with Him. A means He uses to
transform experience.

Sometimes this awareness — that the Bible is a means
we're to use to reach ends that are important to us and to
God — gets lost in a rush to learn some new thing, to defend
a favorite doctrine, or to pinpoint the time of some feature
of Christ's Second Coming according to our interpretation
of eschatology. To new Christians, who aren't up on words
like "doctrine" and "eschatology," the Bible may even sound
so obscure and mysterious that they avoid it, and try to

muddle along on what they can grasp from simplified books
and helpful sermons. It's always dangerous to lose sight of
the fact that the Bible is a Book with a purpose — a Book
given us as a means of Grace, to guide us toward changed
lives.

I suppose I might summarize all this by simply saying,
The Bible is not just for learning, it's for living.

And that secret, the secret of coming to the Bible and
learning for living, is what this book is all about.

Learning for Living

I was excited recently to hear of something I hadn't known
about. Several of my students at Wheaton College's Grad-
uate school had decided to get together to study the Bible
in a reality framework ("reality framework" is the way I
talk about learning for living in my classes). This wasn't
part of my assignment; it grew out of a sense of need to go
beyond "learning a lot about the Bible" to discover Scripture
as God's transforming power in their lives.

When I found out, I asked them to share briefly what the
experience of studying Acts together has meant to them.
I'd like to share what they wrote with you, because their
words capture better than I can express the exciting possibilities that learning God's Word for living holds out.

From Bill

This group has been a blessing for both Carol and me.
We have come to love each member a great deal. The
sharing, reflecting, digging, and applying by the group has
led me to realize the real importance of mutual ministry.
For the past twenty-three years I have led a life in complete darkness. What a joy it is to receive glimpses of truth
as Christ reveals His Word to me, through the eyes and
understanding of the whole group.

The most outstanding point about our group is the fact
that whatever we study in Acts applies to our lives directly.
It's a highlight for me when each of us shares what the
passages say to our lives. We often come to the point where
we give our testimonies, sharing daily problems, and express personal conflicts. This sharing brings the group closer
together and binds us as one in Christ.

The effectiveness of our group doesn't directly rest on

the Bible study alone. The fellowship we have during the rest of the week — at school, in our homes, over the phone — brings the group closer together. We not only relate to each other as persons but we relate Scripture together (this is our support and basis for fellowship). Each of us has the responsibility to memorize parts of the Bible and we are tested during the week by members of the group.

I feel that our group has made a good beginning in its attempt to approach Scripture in a reality framework. I am becoming more aware of my daily life as a committed Christian. I'm applying God's Word to my life and getting support from other Christians who really care that I continue to grow.

From Nancy, this revealing personal reaction:

One advantage of being in a group Bible study is motivational. Reading Acts, knowing that I will be sharing my findings with a group of my peers, makes me begin to dig. And digging is what I need, because I've spent ten odd years letting Scripture "zap" me without making it a part of my everyday life. Somehow I've missed out in learning self-discipline; reading the Scripture and praying especially. Having to share with a group of others has motivated me to consider starting to think about the Scripture — and at least that's a start.

My world is pretty limited looking through one pair of eyes, but boy, when I begin to look through five or six other pairs of eyes, too, things look different. Having five different views of one chapter in Acts is frustrating — but frustrating is not all thumbs-down, if it makes you realize that perhaps there are different angles just as valid as yours. All of a sudden a chink (granted small) falls out of that wall and new light shines in and you're free to be creative and see different ideas. The Holy Spirit has a lot to do with our group interaction too, I'm sure. PRAISE GOD!

Sometimes I'd love to just scream if one more person asks me, "What is Acts 1:8?" But you see, I've committed myself to memorizing the important passages and when I see Barb coming, I review real fast. At least I am memorizing — and finding it useful at other times too (surprise).

Somehow this thing about commitment is real when you have other kids checking up on you! Like I said in front of six other kids that I felt a need to really work on my prayer life — at least an extra thirty minutes of prayer a day. Now that's specific and when someone says, "How's the prayer life?" I gulp and say, "I forgot today," or "It's getting a little easier." But I do appreciate their checking up on me . . . and I always get my chance to check up on them too. I've decided that if I can't live the Christ life in front of them that I'll never do it elsewhere. In spite of all the razzing, a little bit of love and concern for each other breaks through — that's nice.

It's still groovy to be shocked with the reality that Scripture presents life as it really is — like when the new church prayed for boldness and got it — and we prayed for love for each other and *(HEAVENS)* got it!

Whether I'm a hand, a foot, or just a hair on a head, it's goodgoodgood to be part of a body . . . and when one part hurts the hand-foot-or-just-hair hurts too — and when one part sings I hum along too!

From Barb, this description of how the group works:

Through the atmosphere of openness and genuine concern there's the freedom to relax, to speak, to bounce ideas, to discover, to be yourself. Gradual personal revelation results in the context of the passage under study, and sharing flows spontaneously from the discussion of the Scripture. There is no designated leader, though Bill is kind of a guide in some respects, and observations bubble from all at random. When certain points seem to evoke no comment, they are passed over — there is no rigid verse-by-verse analysis. We share what *we* have found — this builds responsibility for digging into the next two chapters so that our discoveries will benefit the group.

The element of commitment was stressed at the group's inception — and this reminder binds us together as in-depth seekers — people who have felt the need for deep fellowship and who have been honest in admitting their need. Thus we have a common bond, and we can work together toward a common goal, beginning to touch God and each other together in a new way, beginning to experience the form of His body, beginning to recognize and exercise our spiritual gifts. We are all givers, not merely receivers, receptive and able to give. Maybe I'll learn more of what Christian love encompasses — a real giving of myself to other believers consistently.

Worship is fresh and spontaneous. We see Him in the Scripture, hear of His action in each others lives, and go to Him in community in praise and request. It's meaningful because it arises *from* interaction with His Word and members of His family.

The Bible study is an excellent focus — keeping us looking to Him. Acts is exciting, alive with probing questions that demand a rethinking of church life, a consideration of newness and culture and a re-evaluation of self and present attitudes and life-styles. Memory verses are chosen to key passages which we feel apply most directly to our group. This aids me in learning Scripture, which I have not done enough of — sort of motivational.

Really, I'm anxious to come back after Christmas vacation to share and build some more.

And from another Barb:

When we started we decided to develop a Wednesday night Bible study group with real commitment involved. This commitment bit is important to me. Not one Wednesday evening since we started have I really felt that I could take the time from my studies to go to Bible study. But I couldn't not go either.

I am convinced that the reason I'm in grad school here is not primarily to cram my head with some knowledge about the Bible. I think I am here because God wants me to learn in a fuller way how He is working in people's *lives* and changing the world today. Theory is fun — and I get really excited about how things fit together (for instance how something we learn in Mark fits what we study in Youth Ministry, etc.). But what excites me more is realizing that we aren't just studying about the church — the body of Christ — we *are* the body of Christ.

There are certain things I've begun to take for granted since we've been meeting. For one, I just assume that these people really are interested in me as a person. If someone asks me, "How are you?" I am in the habit of not answering. But if Bill or Barb or Nancy or one of the other people in the group ask me the same question, I assume they mean it. And I think this assumption is well founded. Then, too, I tend not to just say "Hi" if I see one of the members of our little group — I want to know what is happening in their lives. I also assume that sometime in the ensuing week Bill is going to stop me and ask, "What's Acts 5:29?" (or whatever verses we decided to memorize that week).

But one of the most important things for me is that I am beginning to assume that God is really working in us —

21

and I find myself expectantly watching to see what is happening.

I do not see small groups as necessarily the answer to all the world's problems. But I do know that right now these people who are praying for me, supporting me, loving me are people whom I trust and love with my very being. But God *is* using them to change me, although it isn't very rapid change. And I can see how others are changing as well — not into a mold, but more free to become ourselves. And I have found that the interest I have in them, and how God is working in their lives, is important for my vision of the world.

I really love them.

And *that* is pretty neat.

Learning, Together

It's exciting to me to see God at work in the lives of people who study His Word together. Barb and Nancy and the others are beginning to taste and see how good God is — how good it is to open our hearts to each other and to the transforming, Living Word. It's exciting for me as I write this to realize that what they've begun to find is actually there, in Scripture, awaiting every believer. For it truly is. Exactly those experiences Bill and the girls tell of are open to us all . . .

Looking at the Bible through other pairs of eyes.

Discovering that Scripture applies directly to our lives.

Applying the Word, and getting support from other Christians who really care that you continue to grow.

Experiencing Christian love.

Experiencing Christ's Body.

Seeing change, in your life, and in others.

Sensing worship arise from interaction with God's Word and with other members of His family.

Knowing God in a fresh way, at work in your life.

I hope that a sense of need for experiences like these led you to pick up this book. That the desire to know God's Word in a fresh and living way so grips you that you're ready to go on, now, with others, to develop a fellowship of love in mutual commitment to the God who speaks out vibrantly in Scripture. Ready to come with them to the Bible, seeking new life in Him.

FOLLOW THROUGH

1. *Individual before meeting:* to prepare for your first time together, read over the four reports of shared Bible study in this chapter, and underline anything that reflects your hopes for this study time together.

   When you meet: spend an hour or so sharing your hopes. Particularly share any experiences that have helped you realize your need for studying the Bible and sharing your life with others.

   Look on this first time together as an opportunity to build an understanding of members of your group — a chance to become sensitive to each one's hopes and fears for your fellowship.

2. *Individual before meeting:* look over the procedures outline (Figure 1) developed by the young people quoted in the chapter. You may want to adopt or alter their approach, but it will be important for your group to make some "ground rule" decisions this first time. Check back over what each participant has written, to discover the role each item on their agenda played in the life of the group.

3. *When you meet:* share your reactions to the approach outlined, and work toward a consensus decision on your own commitments and procedures. Note two things. (1) A consensus decision is one that all members of the group agree is the best under the circumstances — not a decision all think is ideal. (2) Your meetings should probably be weekly. You'll find you need regular and frequent sharing to develop awareness of your oneness in Christ.

4. *When you meet:* with decisions made, begin now to pray for one another, showing particular concern for the hopes and uncertainties each one has expressed.

Bible Study Group

Purpose:

It is the purpose of this group to approach Scripture in a reality structure framework. We each have a lack of Bible content and a desire to apply Bible truths to our lives.

Procedures:

Our Wednesday night study follows this format:
I. Fellowship (time varies)
   A. Informal sharing of what has been happening in our lives.
   B. Follow-up on application goal set last week.
II. Prayer
III. Bible study
   A. Sections studied inductively.
   B. Parallel Scriptures studied and discussed.
   C. General sharing and revealing from lives in light of the passages studied.
IV. Memory Verses
   A. Select key verses group will memorize.
   B. Group quizzes each other during week.
V. Applications
   Each member shares what they hope to apply during the week.
VI. Group prayers
VII. Informal fellowship continues

Figure 1

The plan and procedure followed by those quoted
in chapter one for their "learning together" sessions.

Principles

1. The Bible is given us for our transformation.
2. God *never* speaks to believers in tones of Law.

Section One:
PERSPECTIVE

In Bondage

The Bible presents a grim picture of
human bondage. Sin, working in believer
and unbeliever alike, makes us unable
to live by God's standards. It's important
to remember that God speaks to us in
view of our bondage. He doesn't tell us
what we "ought" to do. He doesn't urge
us on to greater efforts. The Christian is
"not under Law" — and grasping this
principle is a vital key to transforming
Bible study:
**God never speaks to believers in
tones of Law.**

In a now famous book, *Games People Play*, Dr. Eric Berne
has pointed out that "in their family and business relationships, most people are constantly playing games with each
other. What's more, they are striving — often unconsciously
— for an emotional 'payoff' which is startlingly different from
what they might rationally expect to get from winning or
losing their game." [1]

In his book Dr. Berne describes some of the hidden motives and desires which motivate and move us, and notes
our "basic dishonesty" in our attempts to satisfy them. He
points out that we could, feeling the need for reassurance,
simply ask for it. Instead, our common approach is to attempt to *maneuver* others into a place of disadvantage where
we can force them to do what we feel we want. [2] It's this,
life lived with others as a set of maneuvers rather than honest
expressions of our feelings and our needs, that Dr. Berne
labels "games."

And it is this, the unconscious and utterly normal dishonesty of our relationship with ourselves and others, that
illustrates the bondage in which we live, the sinfulness

[1] Eric Berne, *Games People Play*, New York: Grove Press, Inc., 1967,
p. 1.
[2] *Op. cit.*, p. 48.

which limits us and which we must face before we can clear off that standing place from which to discover the Bible as God's living Word. For God's Word speaks to us *as we are*. And we *are* in bondage: we *are*, in ourselves, helpless to live life freely and honestly.

It's striking, in reading Dr. Berne's descriptions of 120 of the most common maneuvers and motives, to hear such blaring echoes of Scripture. As portrait after portrait of deceit is sketched and analyzed one sees ever more sharply the Scripture's evaluation of those who have no real hold on the truth: "Disputation and argument, things which lead to nothing but jealousy, quarreling, insults and malicious innuendos — continual wrangling" (1 Tim. 6:3f). "But what about the feuds and struggles that exist among you?" asks the Bible. "Where do they come from? Can't you see that they arise from conflicting passions within yourselves? You crave for something and don't get it; you are murderously jealous of what others have got and what you can't possess yourselves; you struggle and fight with one another" (James 4:1).

Both experience and Scripture testify that this morbid jumble is our heritage. That sin, which twists and taints every man, expresses itself not only in rebellion against God but in the fetidness and frustration of a life lived in the grip of uncontrollable desires. The Bible also calls this bondage death: "being . . . spiritually dead all the time that you drifted along on the stream of this world's ideas of living, and obeyed its unseen ruler (who is still operating in those who do not respond to the truth of God)" (Eph. 2:1f). It may be difficult to accept, but before the Word of God can bring us life, we must permit it to kill. We cannot "deny a truth that you must recognize in your inmost heart" — that in ourselves we are bound, under the control of this world, of our own evil nature, of Satan himself (James 3:13f). Twisting away from this truth is only one evidence of our bondage; only another "maneuver" that forces us further into the helplessness of self-deceit. Because we *are* bound and helpless we must face our helplessness before we can find freedom to run.

The Law Game

How we play it. It's striking that in our maneuvering we even use Scripture to deny Scripture. Our most common attempt to deny our helplessness is to appeal to God's commands, and to insist that "ought implies can."

This is an easy game to play. You page through the Bible until you find a statement like one which Jesus made to Israel in His early sermons: "You must change your hearts — for the kingdom of Heaven has arrived" (Matt. 4:12f). Then you say triumphantly, "See! I *can* change my own heart, or this command would be meaningless. Since I *can* act, I am certainly not helpless. I am certainly not bound. I *must* be free!" And then you settle back into bondage, pretending the chains are gone.

It's easy to demonstrate that this is only a game; a maneuver we undertake to blind ourselves to the truth. How? Put the argument to the test of experience. Try to change yourself. *No man who has claimed the ability to change his own heart has ever done so!*

No man can.

Even though people who dare to try find it impossible to respond fully to the command of Law, they still play the game. They say, "Well, maybe I can't do it now . . . (suggesting it was because "I had a cold at the time, and I get very irritable when I have a cold" or making some other excuse that comes easily to mind) . . . I can do it later." Or, "*someone* can do it." In this game, if *anyone* can even potentially win, all win. Because then no one would have to admit utter helplessness.

It should be clear that there's something wrong with a game in which the manipulation of ideas is allowed to pass for life. In the first chapter I suggested that what we all yearn for is reality we can experience as whole persons — that we long to see ourselves actually becoming. If this is true, the one arena in which all "truths" must prove themselves is life. And the only playing field we should be willing to admit is that provided by life itself. Yet people who play the Law game, when their maneuvering and posturing is found empty of power to change life, retreat to the world of ideas and struggle ever so hard to settle back uncomfortably into blindness. But even in the world of ideas the attempt to play a game with God's Law is an empty one. For the Bible clearly teaches that God's command is no call to pretend: it is a call to confession.

"Law keeps slipping into the picture," the Bible says, "to point out the vast extent of sin" — not to reassure us of imagined human ability (Rom. 5:20). It is this the Bible speaks of when it says that "the law is good in itself and has a legitimate function; yet we know that the Law is not really meant for the good man, but for the man who has neither principles nor self control" (1 Tim. 1:5f). What does the Law do then? If the command, with its powerful Ought, does not imply "can" and urge on us greater efforts to free ourselves, what does it do for us and to us? Put simply, it kills us.

"When the commandment arrived," the apostle Paul says, "sin sprang to life and I 'died.' The commandment which was meant to be a direction to life, I found was a sentence to death. . . . Can it be that something that is intrinsically good could mean death to me? No, what happened was this. Sin, at the touch of the Law, was forced to expose itself as sin, and *that* meant death for me. The contact of the Law showed the sinful nature of sin" (Rom. 7:7f).

The Law sets no goal toward which we must struggle, and it was never meant to. The Law is a measuring rod, and when we stand up straight against it it destroys all our pretenses, crushes our foolish posturings, and lays our hopes to final rest by revealing the vast extent of our bondage and the totality of our helplessness. The powerful Ought of God's Law comes not to reassure, but to terrify — to force us to abandon our pitiful maneuvering and honestly face who we are.

Why do we play? Why do we play it, then, this game with Law? Why do we resist so desperately Scripture's revelation of our bondage?

Partly, perhaps, because however dark the pit, we can still see the stars. We can look up, beyond ourselves, and yearn. We can long to become. The potential of the image of God that is, with sin, our heritage, is always with us, shouting its mute testimony and refusing to let us be satisfied with what we are. The ideal is there.

But so is the reality. And it's the reality we dare not hold up to the light. So we play, to hide our shame. "This is the judgment," the Word proclaims, "that light has entered the world and men have preferred darkness to light because their deeds are evil. Anybody who does wrong hates the light and keeps away from it, for fear his deeds may be exposed" (John 3:19f). So far we've viewed our human condition as a bondage in which we lie helpless. This passage points out that there is a dimension not revealed by the symbolism of chains. That dimension is one of choice. Men have "preferred" darkness to light. We "hate the light, and keep away from it." We "fear exposure." In choosing bondage over the honest exposure of our shame-filled condition, we shoulder the added burden of guilt.

These two compelling motives keep us struggling to hold Law at arms length; lest it burst through our defenses to strip away every pretense and reveal us, hopelessly lost, choking in our own guilt and shame.

How tragic that we don't understand. For only in accepting death wielded by the Law can we find life. Only in exposure is there hope for God to open our eyes, to turn us from darkness to light, "from the power of Satan to God himself, so that they may know forgiveness of their sins and take their place with all those who are made holy by their faith in me [Christ]" (Acts 26:18). In exposing ourselves and facing honestly who we are, we become ready to accept forgiveness.

The man who cannot admit his sin must always deny his need for forgiveness.

And find himself cut off from life.

Exposure

It's surprising to realize, I suppose, that our guilt and shame are greater barriers to us than to God. Knowing us as we really are, God does not shrink back, but reaches out. It is we who draw back; we who are unwilling to face ourselves.

In some of us, maneuvering to avoid exposure is unconscious. We are not aware of it. To others pretense and self-righteousness are a way of life.

The Bible gives us illustrations of both kinds of men and

their response to Law. The "rich young ruler" was a sincere man. We see him in Scripture running up to Jesus, to fall at His feet and ask, "What must I do to be sure of eternal life?"

In responding, Jesus used the Law. "You know the commandments," He returned, listing those of the Ten that concerned responsibilities to other men. "Do not murder, Do not commit adultery, Do not steal, Do not bear false witness, Do not cheat, Honor thy father and mother."

" 'Master,' he replied, 'I have carefully kept all these since I was quite young.'

"Jesus looked steadily at him, and his heart warmed toward him. Then he said: 'There is one thing you still want. Go and sell everything you have, give the money away to the poor — you will have riches in Heaven. And then come back and follow me.' "

And the Bible tells us, "At these words the man's face fell and he went away in deep distress, for he was very rich" (Mark 18:17f).

The sincere among us are like this. We honestly do our best to live up to the standards we feel the Law sets. We work carefully at keeping all these from the time we are quite young. And so, except for a nagging uncertainty that keeps us from being "sure of eternal life," we console ourselves that we are doing quite well. Certainly as well as can be expected.

But as we search the Scripture in our sincerity, we always come on at least one standard by which we know we fall short. In the case of the young ruler, it was a commandment Jesus had not specified: Thou shalt have no other gods before Me. Unknown to himself, this young man had another God — his wealth. When the two gods met in conflict, he chose to serve cash, not Christ.

He went away "in deep distress," but he did go away.

In this both his bondage and his choice of bondage were made clear: Law had spoken its condemning Word.

 It is doubtful that he heard. He went away. And, if he was like the rest of us, he redoubled his efforts to live up to those standards he felt he might reach, and tried to hide from himself the one great failure that, if honestly faced, would expose his guilt and his shame.

Other men, modeled in the New Testament Pharisee, choose conscious pretense. They pay strict attention to the minutia of Law, are fond of cleansing the outside of cups and dishes, while inside they are "full of greed and wickedness." They pray — in public where they can be admired. They give generously to charity — on street corners, preceeded by men who pound on drums to gather an admiring crowd to witness their act of generosity. And they hate other men, looking down on them with a sneer. Not even struggling against the basest of motives, they self-righteously hide from themselves behind pious masks. They even feel confident enough to present a mask to God, as Jesus illustrated in His story of those who were confident in their own goodness and looked down on others in Luke 18.

To make either response to Law, the sincere attempt or the hypocritical pretense, is a disaster for us. At best either can only hold off despair.

But it is to just this despair that God designed Law to drive us!

For Christ's words are utterly true: everyone who sets himself up as somebody will become a nobody. Only the man who makes himself a nobody has the slightest chance of becoming somebody.

ADVENTURE

When you come together to share this week you'll probably want to discuss some of the ideas presented in this chapter. But before you do, spend some time sharing your experiences. It's really true: ideas take on meaning in the context of life. Your discussion will be much more significant if you work first on understanding one another as whole persons.

EXPLORATION 1

Chat with one other person and together develop a list of things you have been taught, as a Christian, in an "ought" framework. (For example, "A Christian ought to witness.")

EXPLORATION 2

Share these with the whole group, and select an item you have listed in common. Then imagine yourselves

33

in a situation in which you suddenly feel, "Now I really ought to . . ." (do the thing you've chosen).

At that moment, how do you *feel?* Jot down a few key words, then share them with the group.

A moment later, if you have failed to do it, how do you feel? Again jot down key words, and discuss them.

A moment later, if you did it, how do you feel? Jot down key words, discuss.

EXPLORATION 3

Look at the key words your group has come up with in exploration 2. Would you encourage a person to become a Christian so he could have the joy of experiencing these feelings?

What has this exploration activity shown you about the nature of Law? About your own relationship with God?

EXPLORATION 4

In chapter two the author discusses two responses to Law, typified by the rich young ruler and the Pharisee. Look over the description of each on pages 32, 33, and try to "get inside their skin." That is, let your imaginations loose, and together build a picture of each man: his feelings, his attitudes, his ways of looking at life, his ways of relating to others, his feelings about himself.

Principles

1. The Bible is given us for our transformation.
2. God *never* speaks to believers in tones of Law.
3. God's words are words of Gospel.

3
Invaluable

We've just spoken of Law. What about Grace? You'll meet Grace in this chapter, in words like these. "The Bible presents a new basis for relationship: one that avoids the question of merit and performance completely. 'Not by works of righteousness which we have done, but according to His mercy He saved us' (Titus 3:5) are words of Gospel. They reflect God's decision to **disregard performance completely. To choose** to love us."

We need to read Scripture from this perspective, remembering always that **God's words are words of Gospel.**

Just now as my wife came into our apartment from the pool by our front door, the manager dropped a remark, "You're supposed to bring a towel to the pool so you can keep the carpets dry."

This word of law hurt. It hurt, because whatever the intention, it constituted an attack — an attack on my wife's basic sense of worth. All such statements as "you're supposed to" are felt by us in this way. They seem to evaluate us. They seem to weigh us. And they seem to shout out that we have been found wanting.

The feeling that our worth as a person is under attack is a third motive underlying our desperate attempts to play the Law game, described in the last chapter. Somehow we feel that to admit our bondage, to face up to guilt and shame, will destroy us and deny our value. No wonder we resist the condemning Word of Law and struggle to reinterpret it!

In fact, God's Law does *not* attack our worth. Our feelings in this case are totally wrong; totally out of harmony with reality. For *we are valuable because of who we are, not because of what we do.*

In a recent book [1] I've written of two ways in which to establish relationships with other persons. One is a relationship built on *performance*. A performance relationship is illustrated by an employer and employee. Each has certain duties expected of him. The employee is to give a certain amount of time to his job, work hard, follow directions, and in general act as an honest workman. The employer in return is expected to pay his salary, treat him with respect and consideration, and take responsibility for the business that supports both. As long as each performs acceptably, the relationship can continue. But if either fails to perform, the basis of the relationship is destroyed, and it is in danger of breaking down.

Any relationship can have a performance base. A woman who lacks self-confidence may unconsciously choose a domineering husband to protect her from the world she fears. If his apparent strength is later discovered to be weakness, and she is forced into those responsibilities she chose him to avoid, the relationship is in danger of breaking up. Its basis was a performance one, and failure to meet expectations threatens to destroy it.

Nearly all human relationships have a performance base. This is demonstrated by Berne's description of the games people play! We all feel, deep down, that we have to maneuver and manipulate. That if people knew us and our motives in stark reality, we would be rejected. Even the mother who staunchly stands by a son sentenced for some terrible crime commonly insists, "But he's really a good boy!" She feels compelled to find some merit in him to explain her continued love.

The Bible presents another basis for relationship: one that avoids the question of merit and performance completely. "Not by works of righteousness which we have done, but according to his mercy he saved us" (Titus 3:5 KJV) are words of Gospel. They reflect God's decision to *disregard performance entirely.* To *choose* to love us.

God's choice has no reference to any "works of righteous-

[1] The book is *How Do I Fit In?*, published by Moody Press in 1970. It is designed to help young people build the pattern of their own personal relationships on the "acceptance" model given us in Christ rather than on the "performance" models all around us.

ness" which we may have done: it is based solely in God's declaration of our worth in His eyes. He loves us in spite of our utter helplessness to "do anything" to earn His care.

We can see this in Paul's discussion of salvation in Romans:

> What happens now to human pride of achievement? There is no more room for it. Why, because failure to keep the Law has killed it? Not at all, but because the whole matter is now on a different plane — believing instead of achieving. . . .
>
> Now how does all this affect the position of our ancestor Abraham? Well, if justification were by achievement he could quite fairly be proud of what he achieved — but not, I am sure, proud before God. For what does the Scripture say about him?
>
> And Abraham believed God, and it was reckoned unto him for righteousness.
>
> Now if a man *works,* his wages are not counted as a gift but as a fair reward. But if a man, irrespective of his work, has faith in him who justifies the sinful, then that man's *faith* is counted as righteousness, and that is the gift of God.
>
> Romans 3:27f; 4:1f

What does this mean for us? This: Law raises no threat to our sense of worth. Law speaks of performance — "that every excuse may die on the lips of him who makes it, and no living man may think himself beyond the judgment of God. 'No man can justify himself before God' by a perfect performance of the Law's demands — indeed it is the straightedge of the Law that shows us how crooked we are" (Rom. 3:19f). Law does *not* speak of our worth or value to God.

Law merely convinces us that we cannot perform: the Gospel brings us the good news that we are important anyway!

To understand this is to come a long way in our attempt to clear off a place to stand, a place from which we can hear God's Word as a Living Word.

Brought to Self-acceptance

God's way of relating to us in Christ gives us a pattern for all our relationships, including our relationship with ourselves. God's way, to ignore our inability to perform and to accept us as worthwhile and valuable persons in spite of it, the way of unconditional love, is to become our way.

Recently I spoke with a desperate mother. She found it impossible to relate to her teen-age son, and any time they attempted to talk there developed, against their wills, an angry fight. For several months they had lived in the same house, had seen each other daily, and had not spoken. The battles were too painful for each of them.

How had it begun? The boy appeared at the table with dirty fingernails. The mother was concerned — she didn't want her son to grow up to be dirty. So she insisted he get up and clean them before he ate. The next meal she looked first at the nails. They were dirty again! Soon those dirty nails became the focus of their relationship: she, constantly nagging at him to clean them; he, more and more deeply resenting something that seemed to him petty and unimportant. She told herself that her only motive was love — but she communicated to him a demand that he *earn* her love. That he perform up to her standards, or her love would be withdrawn.

However important clean fingernails may be in the ultimate scheme of things, we can perhaps realize that it's more important to communicate love. To let people we love know that we care for *them* — not for manipulating them, using them, or pushing them to live up to our standards. It's particularly important because all of us fear that the love of those we care about is, at heart, conditional love.

We have reason to fear. That is the way we ourselves love, conditionally. For there's an important difference between conditional and unconditional love. Unconditional love is utterly realistic, seeing its object as it really is, and loving anyway.

Remember the saying of Jesus which I quoted earlier? "Thou shalt love thy neighbor as thyself." Well, we can *only* love our neighbor as we love our self. If we can't accept ourselves as we really are, in our bondage and helplessness, we can never love our neighbor as he is. We will always love conditionally; we will always seek some performance on his part as the basis for continued relationship. This will be the only way of relating to others that we can emotionally grasp and understand. So it is important that we learn to love ourselves as we are.

But dare we love ourselves unconditionally? Is it right to look at what Law exposes us to be, dead in sin and choosing sin, and to *love?*

YES!

This is the whole point!

"We can see that it was while we were powerless to help ourselves," the Bible says, "that Christ died for sinful men . . . the proof of God's amazing love is that it was *while we were sinners* that Christ died for us" (Rom. 5:6f). God loves us as we are.

In my wife's jewel box is a pair of tarnished earrings, each clasping a tiny chip of cheap green glass. They're worthless to anyone but her. She treasures them as the shyly offered gift a six-year-old gave his teacher because of love. It's God's love that transforms us too . . . into a treasure.

How "valuable" are we? Invaluable.

Beyond the cost of God's Own Son.

The Christian, then, lives asserting both his helplessness and his essential worth. He loves himself, not because of what he is, but in spite of it. He accepts himself for what he is, because God accepts him. And in taking this stand on God's Word he begins to discover that it is a Living and transforming Word indeed.

Later we'll see how the Word transforms, and how acceptance and love for ourselves as sinners doesn't lead us to settle down into self-satisfaction. For now just this one thing is important. That we do love ourselves, unconditionally. That we begin to experience self-acceptance, that amazing ability to look honestly at ourselves, and yet to assert joyfully that we are important, that we are worthwhile, that we are, in fact, beyond valuing.

Brought to Freedom From Law

So far in this chapter I have argued that the hurt which Law's demanding "you're supposed to . . . " seems to inflict stems from a tragic misunderstanding of reality. With our perception distorted by our bondage to sin, we have mistakenly associated our worth as persons with our ability to perform. It is as if we were some circus beast, whose value goes up with skill in the ring and disappears when that ability is impaired. But we are men, created by God "a little lower than the angels" and with a destiny far beyond theirs. Our value has no relationship to our performance.

This remains true for us all our lives. God doesn't give us His new life on condition that we perform after we receive it. Whatever His salvation does, it does not change our essential helplessness. "Without me you can do nothing," Christ told His disciples. We continue to be sinners; we continue in constant need of His power to lift us beyond ourselves.

It's important to accept this fact — to learn to depend on it. Shifting relationship with God back toward a performance base only cuts us off from the transformation we yearn for. As the apostle John warned his readers,

> . . . if we are really living in the same light in which he eternally exists, then we have true fellowship with each other, and the blood which his Son shed for us keeps us clean from all sin. If we refuse to admit that we are sinners, then we live in a world of illusion and truth becomes a stranger to us. But if we freely admit that we have sinned, we find God utterly reliable and straightforward — he forgives our sins and makes us thoroughly clean from all that is evil.
>
> (1 John 1:5f)

Willingness to take our place as needy sinners frees God to forgive, and to act to "make us thoroughly clean from all that is evil." And this leads us to a question.

How then do we stand with Law?

The answer (our blind compulsion to find a performance basis for relationships makes it hard for us to grasp this) is: We have *no* relationship to Law. Law, for the Christian, is a dead and useless thing.

Law's function is fulfilled. We've seen what that function was. Law "keeps slipping into the picture to point out the vast extent of sin"; that "every excuse may die on the lips of him who makes it." Law is designed to bring us to face ourselves, force us to admit the bondage and guilt it exposes . . . *and nothing else!*

This is why Paul wrote to the Galatians,

. . . while we were "children" we lived under the authority of basic moral principles. But when the proper time came God sent his Son, born of a human mother and born under the jurisdiction of Law, that he might redeem those who were under the authority of the Law and lead us into becoming, by adoption, true sons of God.

(Gal. 4:3-5)

Bought by Christ out from under Law's jurisdiction, honestly confessing the helplessness Law exposes, and finding through faith in the Gospel a basis for relationship with God that has nothing to do with performance, we have no more need of Law. The Bible asks, "Are we then undermining the Law by this insistence on faith? Not a bit of it! We put Law in its proper place" (Rom. 3:31).

Really, it's exciting. To realize that Law (which hurt us so much and made us feel so guilty in our inability to perform) has no more power over us. We have admitted everything the Law exposes. We've taken our place, guilty before the Judge. And we've discovered that we are still valued, still important, still loved.

We never have to hide again.

And this frees us from Law. Law was designed to grind our masks to dust. When we take off our masks, gladly expose ourselves as we really are, Law's hammer blows stop. Law has no more business with us.

Law's ability is limited. This is the second great reason why the Christian is free from the Law. Law produced awareness of guilt; it *never* produced transformation. We still try to use Law in our becoming, a natural hangover from our old ways of thinking. But it never works.

"O you dear idiots," Paul wrote to the Galatians when they tried to make use of Law as a guidepost to Christian living,

. . . who has been casting a spell over you? I shall ask you one simple question: Did you receive the Spirit by trying to keep the Law or by believing the message of the gospel? Surely you can't be so idiotic as to think that a man begins his spiritual life in the Spirit and then completes it by reverting to outward observances? Has all your painful experience brought you nowhere? I simply cannot believe it of you! Does God, who gives you his Spirit and works miracles among you, do these things because you

INVALUABLE

41

have obeyed the Law or because you have believed the Gospel? Ask yourselves that.

(Gal. 3:1f)

This is an "idiocy" toward which we're all prone, this attempt to go on toward spiritual maturity through obedience to Law. But it isn't the way God works. The Gospel is based on other dynamics entirely.

Law's voice is within us. This is why at times our freedom escapes us. Once Law has done its work, creating despair, forcing us to face ourselves, it is done with us. God's Word no longer comes to us as Law.

Later we'll see that even the most definite command is no longer Law but can be heard as Good News. For now, let's simply note this again: *the essence of legalism is the idea that we are called on to perform.*

To hear God's Word as a demand for performance is a retreat to Law, and this makes Scripture a killing thing, powerless to make alive.

Perhaps we can understand why. "While we were 'in the flesh,'" the Bible says, "Law stimulated our sinful passions and so worked in our nature that we became productive — for death" (Rom. 7:5f). That is, when we listened to Law state its expectations, we were motivated to action. But we can't live up to the expectations stated. So our energy is forced into maneuvering, into manipulating, into making and hiding behind masks. Unwilling simply to admit our bondage and our shame, we struggle and act and choose — sin — and gain only guilt.

Any Word of God can be heard by us as Law, even the Gospel itself. "Believe on the Lord Jesus Christ" is, to some people, just the opposite of an invitation to life: it is an oppressive command, and they struggle against it, demanding to know "why do I *have to* believe?"

So the Law is always with us, within our own personality. Law is with us as our natural inclination to interpret Scripture legalistically; our tendency to build up little human codes and sets of regulations which we can pretend are "living the Christian life." How freeing the True Word is when it comes: "While we were in the flesh the Law . . . but now that we stand clear of the Law . . . we are free to serve God. Not in the old obedience to the letter of the Law, but in a new way, in the Spirit."

And we are free.

"For the new spiritual principle of life 'in' Christ Jesus lifts me out of the old vicious circle of sin and death" (Rom. 8:2). It is in being lifted out that we can experience a Living Word.

ADVENTURE

Saint *and* sinner, helpless in bondage yet inexpressibly valuable, it's no wonder we often have such ambivalent feelings about ourselves. Recognizing both poles of being a person, accepting ourselves as who we are, is a basic step toward becoming who we are in Christ.

EXPLORATION 1

In chapter three the author suggests a Christian is free to make twin assertions: an assertion of his helplessness, and an assertion of his worth. But it is hard to see ourselves honestly, without masks. To explore your perception of yourself, take crayons and a large sheet of paper and draw yourself "as you really are." Try to represent your real self, as you understand yourself right now.

EXPLORATION 2

If you choose to, share these pictures with each other.

EXPLORATION 3

Read together and discuss Romans 7:7 - 8:8, sharing particularly any ways in which the Word captures your own experience or speaks of something important to you.

Principles

1. The Bible is given us for our transformation.
2. God *never* speaks to believers in tones of Law.
3. God's words are words of Gospel.
4. God never speaks or acts contrary to His love for us.

4

A God of Love

In a very vital way, our transformation
depends on growth in relationship with
God. When we learn to trust God completely, and to rest in the fact that God
is love, we've come a long way in finding
the Bible to be a Living Word for us.

Developing this confidence is often hard
for us. But it's possible, if we learn to
interpret our experiences, and God's words,
through the love of God demonstrated
to us in Jesus Christ.

Put as a principle to guide us in Bible
study we might state it this way: **God never
speaks or acts contrary to His love for us.**

One of the hardest things for an untrustworthy man to
do is to trust. When a person's whole life style, consciously
or unconsciously, is one of manipulation and posturing, it's
hard to believe that the face another person presents is
real.

Perhaps this is why many of us find it hard to trust God.
Like the young college student who shared with me his fear
and horror that God might force him to go to the mission
field, we're never quite sure that God's involvement in our
lives is really good.

We can see why. We can see the reason in a young wife
who, never experiencing selfless love in her childhood home,
feeling betrayed by a weak father who would not defend
her from a bitter and critical mother, found herself empty
of the ability to trust and to love. Trust and love are qualities so foreign to us that we need a model to understand
them; we need to experience them before we can take our
own first tentative steps to extend them to others. So, knowing only our own untrustworthiness, experiencing only the
failure of others to keep our trust, we have great difficulty
in trusting God.

We fall into the trap of creating God in our own image;

of imagining motives behind His actions that are as self-centered and pitiless as we know our own can be.

This trap is easy to recognize, but it's hard to avoid. Whatever the arguments and however hard we try to convince ourselves, emotionally we hesitate. We draw back. Once again we prove ourselves whole persons; mere intellectual assent to the idea that God is love is not enough. And so we struggle for the freedom to throw our total selves unhesitatingly into the arms of God, abandoning ourselves to His love.

It's hard to say how this freedom comes. I certainly have no formula to offer. I have a suspicion that freedom begins to dawn when we accept ourselves: when we can look honestly at who and what we are, and still feel valuable and worthwhile. Learning to love ourselves, we can perhaps begin to believe, hoping against hope, that God actually means it when He says He loves us; that the life and death and resurrection of Jesus Christ aren't merely moves in some cosmic chess game in which we're meaningless pawns, but are bold moves motivated by unimaginable love, with you and me the treasured prize, to be won or lost. There's a great difference between being a pawn and being a prize. Feeling yourself a pawn, you can never trust. You may be expendable, treated with planned unconcern to gain some strategic advantage. Feeling yourself a prize, you can rest secure. The game isn't played *with* you, but *for* you. It was Christ, the great Sacrifice, who was moved by God across the board of history who was used: it is Christ who proves decisively the love of God and the trustworthiness of God.

But how are we to come to trust?

Self-revelation

I suppose all of us have difficulties in building those more intimate relationships where trust is a key factor. As a young husband I failed to understand one difficulty, and this caused my wife and me years of pain and alienation.

I am a person who finds it hard to express feelings. Comfortable in the world of ideas, I have to struggle to express the emotions, motives, and reactions to others that swirl inside and are such basic elements in every personality. My wife lives much more fully in these realms, and needs to live there. So when marriage brought its usual tensions and strains, its multiplied occasions for misunderstanding, she looked desperately for reassurance and explanation. But my response in such a situation was to retreat, to resist talking our feelings and motives through. It was easier to keep silent or talk ideas — anything to avoid facing a dimension of life with which I felt inadequate to deal.

Over the years I tried in many ways to express love. I told her daily, "I love you." I took on part of the household chores. Against my judgment I bought "foolish" things just because she wanted them. And I was sure that every day the things I did expressed love.

So I was jolted when, after ten years of marriage, I was confronted by a heartbroken wife who was convinced above all else that I did not love her, because I shared everything but my inner self with her.

It was a painful, important lesson. *What I do requires explanation.* Actions can't stand alone; they are made meaningful only by a revelation of the feelings and concerns which motivated them.

Of course the opposite is also true. Expression of feelings is made meaningful by actions. They are demonstrated in the stream of daily life, nowhere else. But when these two, self-revelation and action, harmonize, we are reassured. Together they help us begin to trust.

I share this personal experience for one reason only. The Living Word calls us to a relationship with God. To a person-to-Person intimacy. In this relationship we need to understand and to accept ourselves [the thing I was unable to do as a young husband]. And we need to clarify our vision of God. To feel certain of His feelings and motives. To discover Who this Person is we're invited to trust. To see Him as He really is. The Bible becomes a Living Word for us when we realize that this is its focus: that we might know Christ.

All Scripture points us to Christ. "The Gospel is centered in God's Son," Paul begins the letter to Rome. And throughout Scripture this testimony is repeated. In Christ God "gives a full and complete expression of the invisible God . . . life from nothing began through him, and life from the dead began through him, and he is, therefore, justly called the Lord of all. It was in him that the full nature of God chose to live . . . " (Col. 1:15f).

It is Christ who gives us a solid basis for a trust relationship with God. "God," the writer to Hebrews states, "who gave our forefathers many different glimpses of the truth in the words of the prophets, has now, at the end of the present age, given us the truth in the Son. . . . This Son, radiance of the glory of God, flawless expression of the nature of God, himself the upholding principle of all that is, effected in person the reconciliation between God and man and then took his seat at the right hand of the majesty on high" (Heb. 1:1f). God's personality, His love and concern for man, which could only be glimpsed at a distance through the words of the Old Testament, was fully expressed in warm flesh and coursing human blood.

So we see Jesus.

We see Jesus reaching out to touch a leper when a word could heal. We see Him flare in anger at the hard-heartedness of "religious" men who hesitated at healing on the Sabbath, but did not hesitate to use a cripple as bait to snare the One who was more concerned with human need than with traditions. We see Him crying over Jerusalem, tasting salty tears because men who hated Him were cut off by hate from life. We see Him commanding His disciples to love, and stooping in the dust to wash their feet that they might sense the meaninglessness of pride, and learn to serve. We see Him surrounded by prostitutes and sinful men, who found themselves eager to be near this Person whose holiness somehow drew and did not repel. We see Him, arched painfully on the cross, expending agonized breath to cry, "Father, forgive them!" And we remember the words, "He had loved those who were his in this world, and he loved them until the end."

Flesh and blood expressed in unmistakable form a concern for us that, without an Incarnation, we could only guess at.

Cheap Love?

It's hard to measure the reality and depth of love. My younger children tend to think I love them when I give them whatever they want at the moment. I find I love them most when I refuse. It's a cheap kind of love that does what another wants instead of what's best for him.

Perhaps that's why God's love is often puzzling to us. Even Christ's disciples were puzzled by His love. *How wonderful for us,* they thought, *if He sets up God's Kingdom now. We'll rule with Him.* And they even argued over which of them should have the most important posts in His government. But God's love for us isn't the inferior kind. It insists on the best, even when we can't understand why the best leads to suffering.

It often does. It certainly led Christ there.

It was love that created the cross.

Like His other actions, this culminating act of Christ's life on earth would be easy to misunderstand if it weren't explained. Many misunderstand the cross even with the explanation. They call it weakness, or the bitter but deserved fate of a fool with Messianic delusions. To the Jewish leaders it was a political expedient, ridding Israel of a man who might have upset an uneasy truce with Rome. To Pilate it was a miscarriage of justice, the death of an innocent. But the Bible explains it differently. It was a considered, purposive act, dictated by love.

"What we actually see is Jesus, after being made temporarily inferior to the angels (and so subject to pain and death), *in order that he should, by God's grace, taste death for every man . . .*" (Heb. 2:9f, italics mine). In one of the first sermons after the resurrection Peter would speak of Christ being put into the power of His murderers "by the predetermined plan and foreknowledge of God" (Acts 2: 14f). And Matthew would recall how, when He was betrayed, He rebuked a disciple who drew a sword to defend Him, saying, "Do you imagine that I could not appeal to my Father, and he would at once send more than twelve legions of angels to defend me?" (Matt. 26:47f). God the Father *gave* His Son, and the Son *gave* Himself, in an act that divides time and strikes us mute in silent wonder.

"To us," the Bible says, "the greatest demonstration of God's love for us has been his sending his only Son into the world to give us life through him. We see real love, not in the fact that we loved God, but that he loved us and sent his Son to make personal atonement for our sins. . . . So we have come to know and trust the love God has for us. God *is* love, and the man whose life is lived in love does, in fact, live in God, and God does, in fact, live in him" (1 John 4:7f).

So act and explanation harmonize. Love professed is proven by the ultimate gift of life itself. God the Son tastes the bitterness of sin's alienation; the essence of the Godhead is torn apart, God in agony forsaking God — for us.

That it was for us there is no doubt. He died "to make personal atonement for our sins." Christ "redeemed us from the curse of the Law's condemnation, by himself becoming a curse for us when he was crucified" (Gal. 3:6f). "Through him, at the cost of his own blood, we are redeemed, fully forgiven . . ." (Eph. 1:7). Christ has become our living peace and "by his sacrifice he removed the hostility of the Law, with all its commandments and rules . . . for he reconciled both Jew and Gentile to God by the sacrifice of his body on the cross" (Eph. 2:11f).

The Bible constantly speaks of this great mystery. "If we have, as it were, shared his death, let us rise and live our new lives with him! Let us never forget that our old selves died with him on the cross that the tyranny of sin over us might be broken" (Rom. 6:1f). "Let us grasp the fact that we *have* peace with God through our Lord Jesus Christ. Through him we have confidently entered into this new relationship of grace, and here we take our stand . . ." (Rom. 5:1f). "While we were powerless to help ourselves Christ died for sinful men . . . the proof of God's amazing love is this: that it was *while we were sinners* that Christ died for us. Moreover if he did that for us while we were sinners, now that we are men justified by the shedding of his blood, what reason have we to fear the wrath of God? If, while we were his enemies, Christ reconciled us to God by *dying for us,* surely now that we are reconciled we may be perfectly certain of our salvation through his *living in us*" (Rom. 5:6f). "Just as surely as it is appointed for all men to die once, and after that pass to their judgment, so it is certain that Christ was offered once to bear the sins of men and after that, to those who look for him, he will appear a second time, not this time to deal with sin, but to bring to full salvation those who eagerly await him" (Heb. 9:27f).

I can't explain just how the cross accomplishes all this.

How it channels forgiveness, snatches us out from under Law's condemnation, frees us from the tyranny of our own sin-ridden selves, reconciles us to God, creates a relationship with God in which we know peace and full release from any fear of His just wrath. But it took the cross to do it. And through the cross I finally know the extent of His love. He died for me. I am His prize, not His pawn. A Victor in His death, He has won me, and won for me all I have no hope for in myself.

The bondage of sin is broken.

The guilt of sin is gone.

Through Him I rise beyond myself, and become.

A Place to Stand?

In Scripture I find a revelation of two persons: of myself, and of God. When we accept ourselves and when we see Him as a God of love, trust begins to dawn. The Bible no longer comes to us as Law. It speaks God's great message of love in Christ.

I know that in simply stressing "God is Love" I run a risk of misrepresenting God. God is more than love. Even human personalities are complex, an intricate blend of traits and motives operating across a great complex of situations. We can't label a person "flighty" or "cold" or "intellectual" and hope to represent him faithfully, or explain all his actions. *But we can say that in all God does, He never speaks or acts contrary to His love for us.*

We need to keep this in perspective when we think of God and when we search for the Living Word. Love is the foundation of our relationship; something we can always count on as we grow to know better this One who invites us to discover life in Him. For the Bible presents Christ as the center of its message. Seeing Him, it focuses our attention continually on His great act on Calvary. And what is the nature of that act? It is an act of Love.

If we're to see God through Christ, and if we're to know Christ through the cross, we see unveiled a God of Love.

Not only is the love of God the message of the Living Word; the love of God unlocks the Word for us.

All we read we now read through Christ. As sunglasses tint one's view, Christ's love colors every expression of Scripture. This is an important perspective to maintain. The college student I mentioned earlier feared that God would force him into missions against his will. To him God loomed as a "Sovereign Being" with an awesome power to crush beneath Him whomever He might choose. The Bible does reveal God as Sovereign, with the right to choose and to decree. But this Sovereign God we know in Christ as Love. We read each expression of His power through Christ, and fear aroused through Law is, by Grace, transformed to quiet confidence and peace.

I may not understand His choices.

His actions may seem mysterious, even hard.

But knowing God in Christ I know Him as One who acts in love. I learn to trust.

ADVENTURE

Trust is a fragile thing that grows slowly through acquaintance and testing. It is not surprising that most of us find it hard to trust ourselves to another person: to share what we really are. We know they may think less of us, or use what we expose to hurt us. Still, most of us have known someone we have begun to trust.

Our trust relationship with God is something like this too: it begins with fragile trust, as we meet the love of God in Christ: and it grows more trusting when we come to know Him better. Our progressive transformation, our "becoming," is, as the Bible puts it, "a process begun and continued" through faith (Rom. 1:17).

This *Adventure* is designed to explore the kind of faith that takes the form of trust — as we have known it, and as we can know it in relationship with God.

EXPLORATION 1

Think of one time when you felt warm, secure, loved — when you seemed completely protected and at peace. Share with the others the place or person associated with this experience — try to help them feel that time as you felt it, to enter into your experience almost as if they were there.

EXPLORATION 2

Is there anything that seems common to all the experiences just shared? What are the common elements? What insights does discovering them give into the nature of trust?

EXPLORATION 3

In a very real way trust (or "faith," as the Bible calls it) is not something we can create. It's created in us by our experience with a person — by coming to learn that the one we deal with is trustworthy. "Trust," then, does not really focus on our subjective experience (e.g., I "feel" trust). It focuses on the object of trust (e.g., He *is* trustworthy). In our relationship with God, then, the focus can always be kept on Him — not on the way we happen to feel about Him at the moment. The question always is this: "Is God trustworthy?" Not, "Is my faith strong?"

Realizing this, we want to turn our attention to God. What picture of Him do we have? Let's explore it this way:

Read Mark 3:1-7 individually, and observe Jesus closely. How did He act and respond?

Draw "God" just as you drew your real "self" last session, with crayons on paper. Represent what you feel He is really like, as you have just seen Him revealed in Christ.

Share your pictures and explain them to the others.

Principles

1. The Bible is given us for our transformation.
2. God *never* speaks to believers in tones of Law.
3. God's words are words of Gospel.
4. God never speaks or acts contrary to His love for us.
5. God's ability to express His love is unlimited.

5
A God Who Is God

Even the greatest human love is severely
limited — first by our inability fully to
express it, and secondly by our lack of
wisdom in choosing the loving thing to do.
Too often human experience leads us to
doubt God's freedom to love, and He
seems somehow limited, as we are.

But the God of Scripture isn't this kind
of half-way God. We may not understand all His choices, but we are to read
Scripture with the firm conviction that
**God's ability to express His love is
unlimited.**

There's something heartbreaking about powerless love.

A few years ago I spent five frantic days traveling across
West Texas, Oklahoma, and Nebraska for a series of one-day
conventions; my schedule was speaking all day, traveling
hundreds of miles each night. One morning, as the faint
glow of coming dawn seemed to emphasize the loneliness of
the occasional buttes that marked the desert we traveled,
one of my companions, a pastor from Omaha, told me this
story of powerless love.

It happened in front of his home.

He had been home that day with a cold. His sons were
with him; his wife and daughter were shopping. The boys
were excited; mom was going to bring them something (I
can't remember what) that took on that peculiar importance
little gifts have for children. They watched out the window
for the bus, each eager to catch first sight of the shoppers.
Then they were there! Running out of the house, the boys
raced across the street to meet them.

My friend heard the screech of brakes — and the thud of
impact. He reached his oldest son just in time to take him
in his arms, witness a desperate struggle for breath and to
clasp the boy's hand as he died. His neck and breathing

tubes had been crushed. There was nothing anyone could do.

    ✿   ✿   ✿   ✿   ✿   ✿   ✿   ✿

I remembered that story of helplessness as I recalled another incident. A time when Jesus was approached by a man with festering flesh that warned all to shun him as a dead man, a leper. He came to Jesus suffering a death far more lingering than the child's, and called out, "Lord, if You want to, You can make me clean." "Of course I want to . . ." Jesus replied. Of love there was no doubt. But power? The next words, recorded in the very first chapter of Mark's portrait of the Savior, help us realize that the One we meet in Scripture is no man limited as we.

" . . . *be clean!*"

Love wants to.

Jesus can.

Power

This theme of power underlines many of the stories of the gospels. In Mark the early chapters build toward a climactic revelation of it. Jesus is seen standing in a boat, the experienced fishermen who are His disciples cowering before the violence of a storm. Calmly He rebukes the wind and waves: "Hush now! Be still!"

Jesus is seen vaulting over the boat's side, splashing up to a rocky shore, and rushed upon by a madman who terrorizes the area. Suddenly this man whom no bonds can hold kneels before Jesus, and revealing the demonic source of his strength, begs the Lord as Son of God not to torment him but to permit the evil spirits within to infect a nearby herd of pigs. And as the swine rush madly off a cliff into the sea, the man, restored, begs to follow his deliverer.

Jesus is seen being led through swirling crowds in an oriental marketplace toward a dying girl, pausing in the crush to speak to a woman who reached out to touch His clothing. He hears her story, confirms the healing of her hemorrhage of twelve years, and turns back to follow His guide.

Jesus is seen as messengers arrive with news the girl has died. He continues on, reassures the mourners wailing at that home, and disregarding the scornful laughter of those who have seen the child die takes the parents with him into their daughter's room. He takes her hand and with no great show simply says, "Little girl, I tell you to get up."

It's with such measured cadence Mark presents Christ's power: nature bows to this Man, demons tremble before Him, chronic illness loses hold, and death itself concedes defeat.

No helpless love here.

Jesus Christ is Lord.

It's hard for us to grasp this fact of power and learn to rest in Christ as One who is *unlimited.* It was hard for men in His days on earth, His friends as well as His enemies.

His enemies denied His authority over the intangible. Once, when Jesus responded to faith with the reassurance, "My friend, your sins are forgiven," the scribes and Pharisees began to argue and talk of blasphemy. "Who can forgive sins?" they asked. And they answered their own question, "Only God can do that."

> Jesus realized what was going on in their minds and spoke straight to them.
>
> "Why must you argue like this in your minds? Which do you suppose is easier — to say, 'Your sins are forgiven' or to say, 'Get up and walk'? But to make you realize that the Son of Man has full authority on earth to forgive sins — I tell *you*," he said to the man who was paralyzed, "get up, pick up your bed and go home!"
>
> Instantly the man sprang to his feet before their eyes, picked up the bedding on which he used to lie, and went off home, praising God.
>
> (Luke 5:17f)

Charlatans throughout history have claimed special powers over the intangible. The words, "your sins are forgiven," are easy to speak: who can disprove them? But in Christ, for the first time, the claim of absolute authority over the intangible was proven in the world of flesh and blood and rock and stone. The God who works through natural laws laid them aside, and showed plainly Who it is that controls.

Jesus' friends trusted His teaching. They accepted Him as Lord of the intangible. But even they staggered at the thought that *all* things were under His control. When Lazarus fell sick his sisters sent for Christ. When He finally came to them it was four days after Lazarus had been laid in a hillside tomb. Even so the sisters met Him with touching faith.

> "If only you had been here, Lord," said Martha, "my brother would never have died. And I know that, even now, God will give you whatever you ask from him."
>
> "Your brother will rise again," Jesus replied to her.
>
> "I know," said Martha, "that he will rise again in the resurrection in the last day."
>
> "I myself am the resurrection and the life," Jesus told her. "The man who believes in me will live even though he dies, and anyone who is alive and believes in me will never die at all. Can you believe that?"
>
> "Yes, Lord," replied Martha. "I do believe that you are Christ, the Son of God, the one who was to come into the world."
>
> (John 11:21-27)

Even the pain of a brother's death couldn't shake her faith in Christ: she could view the distant resurrection with confident hope.

But what about the *now?*

Just minutes later they climbed the hill to reach the cave where Lazarus lay, and when Jesus spoke the shocking words, "Take away the stone," it was Martha who objected.

"But Lord, he has been dead four days. By this time he will be decaying . . ."

What was Jesus' reply? "Did I not tell you that if you believed, you would see the wonder of what God can do?"

". . . *Lazarus, come out!*"

This is the God we find in the Living Word. Not a God limited to the future, or One interested only in the intangible. Not a God who, like us, is overwhelmed in the solid world of touch and feel by forces beyond control. In God's Word we meet a Christ who cannot be caught in the crush of any circumstance — a God who speaks and acts in our *now* with unquestioned power.

Listen to it again.

Lazarus, come out.

In Christ we meet, for the first time, unlimited Love made fully free by unlimited Power.

God's Love was demonstrated daily in Jesus' life, and any doubts that might remain were settled in Calvary's great climactic Act of Love. Once and for all our fears that Jesus' life on earth was some planned campaign to trick us, some great deceit, are calmed. For the first time we sinful men meet a Man who does not maneuver and manipulate for His hidden advantage. For the first time we meet selfless love.

The power Jesus displayed in life also has a great climactic demonstration. The Act of Resurrection. Here the death of God's Son is transformed from a tragedy of helpless love into a triumph. In the Resurrection reality is unveiled, and we finally learn that the intangible, which seems so fragile, is far more solid than the physical world our senses know. "The Gospel is centered in God's Son," the Bible says, "a descendant of David by human geneology and *patently marked out as the Son of God by the power of that Spirit of holiness which raised him to life again from the dead*" (Rom. 1:2).

> Christ died for our sins, as the Scriptures said he would . . . he was buried and rose again the third day, again as the Scriptures foretold. He was seen by Cephas, then by the twelve, and subsequently was seen simultaneously by over five hundred Christians, of whom the majority are still alive, though some have since died. He was then seen by James, then by all the messengers. And last of all, as if to one born abnormally late, he appeared to me!
>
> (1 Cor. 15:3f)

The Resurrection brings hope into our lives, for it offers final proof that God is able to transform. Earlier I mentioned our bondage, our helplessness in guilt and shame. The Resurrection becomes the "very heart" of the good news, for it cries out that One who is able to infuse new life into a dead body, transforming it to the extent that it is no longer limited by the physical universe, is able to infuse new life into personalities deadened by sin. The Resurrected Christ is *unlimited*. In His new body He walked through solid walls and appeared suddenly in locked rooms before His astonished disciples. In our new life, God's power breaks

A GOD WHO IS GOD

through the intangible bonds of sin-warped personality that hold us helpless, and frees us.

And it is resurrection power, power for a new life, that God makes available to us in Christ. "That power," the Bible says, "is the same divine energy which was demonstrated in Christ when he raised him from the dead and gave him the place of supreme honor in Heaven — a place that is so infinitely superior to any conceivable command, authority, power or control, and which carries with it a name far beyond any name that could ever be used in this world or the world to come."

"God has placed everything under the power of Christ — " (Eph. 1:15f).

Jesus Christ is Lord.

Choice

These twin assertions of a Living Word that God is both all-loving and all-powerful have often been the playthings of philosophers. They set up arguments like this:

If God were all-loving He would never desire suffering. If God were all-powerful, He would be able to prevent suffering. But suffering exists. Tragedies, like the death of the boy I described at the beginning of this chapter, occur daily. So the conclusion is inescapable. God must either be limited in love, or in power. Either He can't do anything about suffering, or He stands aloof and refuses to be bothered.

The argument looks strong. But God isn't limited by our logic.

God cares.

God can.

And God chooses.

The Bible makes it clear that our God is *God*. *He* makes His decisions, not you or I. In Christ we learn His decisions are motivated by Love. In Christ we also learn that He has unlimited power to express love in His actions. *But we also learn that His choices are guided by a wisdom we often cannot understand.* "Consider," Scripture says.

> . . . what have the philosopher, the writer and the critic of this world to show for all their wisdom? Has not God made the wisdom of this world look foolish? For it was after the world in its wisdom had failed to know God,

that he in his wisdom chose to save all who would believe by the 'simplemindedness' of the gospel message. For the Jews ask for miraculous proofs and the Greeks an intellectual panacea, but all we preach is Christ crucified — a stumbling block for the Jews and sheer nonsense to the gentiles, but for those who are called, whether Jews or Greeks, Christ the power of God and the wisdom of God.

(1 Cor. 1:19f)

And in another place we are warned not to be fooled by "philosophy and empty arguments" but to keep a firm hold on Christ. In Christ we discover both love and power, forgiveness and renewal. And we meet a God who is *God:* the initiative in our relationship is His, and He chooses how His love is to be displayed.

"Everything has been put in my hands by the Father," Jesus once told His disciples, "and nobody knows the Son except the Father. Nor does anyone know the Father except the Son — and the men to whom the Son chooses to reveal him." God took the initiative and broke into our world to release us from bondage; yet He was met by doubt and rejection. Man's natural bent to sin expressed itself in unbelief. "He came into his own creation, and his own people would not accept him. Yet wherever men did accept him he gave them power to become the sons of God. These were the men who truly believed in him, and their birth depended not on the course of nature or on any impulse or plan of man, but on God" (John 1:6f).

And this last fact, that all "depends on God," is the final anchor for our trust.

We can't depend on ourselves. In ourselves, we *are* in bondage.

We can depend on the God revealed in Christ: the Christ who meets us in His Word and stamps His image on each thought and phrase.

What is that image?

Just what we've seen. Of Love, and power to express Love. Of strength to choose the course that best expresses love, even when what Love decrees may at times seem hard. We see Christ, and with Christ in view we read His Word.

*　*　*　*　*　*　*　*

It was quiet in the car when my friend finished telling his story. His head was bowed, and even though his voice had held steady, the strain of remembering was clearly there.

And then he spoke again.

"As I held my oldest son and helpless, watched him die, I began to understand a little of the Love of God. God had the power to help. But He stood back. He watched His only Son die in agony — for me."

"In the face of this," the Bible says, "what is left to say? If God is for us, who can be against us? He who did not grudge his own Son, but gave him up for us all — can we not trust such a God . . . ?" (Rom. 8:31f).

We *can* trust Him.

Trust is all we can do.

And, trusting God to be the God we know in Christ, depending fully on Him, we can discover a Living Word.

ADVENTURE

God's love is easy to lose sight of when we're hurt or overwhelmed by circumstances. God understands this totally, and accepts our spontaneous doubts. But we are invited to grow toward trust, as we'll explore in this *Adventure*.

EXPLORATION 1

All of us at times feel crushed by circumstances, in situations utterly beyond our control. Think of a time when you felt this way; helpless, alone, hurt, overwhelmed.

Share it with the others — try to help them enter into your experience almost as if they were there.

EXPLORATION 2

At times like the ones you've been talking of, we all feel the need of support and love: the need to relax and trust ourselves to someone who cares.

This kind of trust is hard for us, although trust is something that grows. Sometimes a tangible experience of support helps us trust, and it gives us an opportunity to express supportive love.

If you wish to try an experiment in tangible trust, here's how. Form a tight circle of five to eight people with one person standing in the center. The person in the middle lets himself topple, and is passed around the circle, body straight but relaxed, by the others. He is passed around and around until he can relax and trust himself to the group.

After all who wish to have experienced this support, take time to share your feelings while in the center.

EXPLORATION 3

Study Acts 4:13-31 together. How was the situation described like experiences you discussed for Exploration 1? How did the response of the young church in this situation demonstrate trust? What basis for trust did these believers seem to have?

EXPLORATION 4

Think of one area in your life in which you need to "let go" and trust God. Share this with the group, trying to communicate the situation to them as you feel it.

Then close, praying for each other, and committing your needs to Christ.

Principles

1. The Bible is given us for our transformation.
2. God *never* speaks to believers in tones of Law.
3. God's words are words of Gospel.
4. God never speaks or acts contrary to His love for us.
5. God's ability to express His love is unlimited.
6. God's Word reveals reality as He alone knows it.

6

In Truth

Today we are bombarded with various
viewpoints on life and morals and how
we should make the many decisions each
of us face daily. To make right decisions
we need desperately to pierce through
the cloud and fog of human philosophies,
and discover reality. We can, when we
come to Scripture understanding another basic principle:
**God's Word reveals reality as He alone
knows it.**

Recently a column copyrighted by the *New York Times*
reported on Dr. Robert L. Wolk's new book, *The Right to
Lie.* Dr. Wolk, a clinical psychologist, argues that we "all
have the right to lie and that every parent should teach his
children the fine art of lying properly."

Why should a "crusading psychologist" come out strongly
for constructive lies as important tools for living in our contemporary world? For one thing, Wolk believes that if children are taught to tell lies, when they do lie they won't
feel "ego-damaging guilt." For another, he believes that in
various situations lies show love — they have the power to
make others feel better than the truth would. And he also
suggests that lies are a sensible way to get ourselves out of
situations that might be painful for us. Lies are sort of aids
in self-preservation. Suggesting that parents take responsibility for guidance in lying, Dr. Wolk believes that even-
tually youngsters can "learn to use lies considerately and
appropriately to cope with the demands of reality."

What interests me in this isn't the idea that we "ought"
to lie. Or even that we teach lying to our children. I've
run across both thoughts before. What's interesting is the
final justification Wolk seems to give. In one phrase he has
exposed the real issue involved. That phrase? "To cope with
the demands of reality."

Reality is always the issue. The way we behave is always finally based on our perception of what life is really like.

My young daughter takes a strange delight in passing other cars. Whenever we draw up on a motorist ahead her eyes shine, and excitedly she demands, "Pass him, daddy! Pass him!" Cars may be coming on the road ahead, but she still demands, "Pass him!" I try to explain then why I can't. That other cars are coming, that we just can't go *through* that solid hurtling bulk, and certainly would crash. But she doesn't understand, and she cries louder, "Pass him, daddy! Pass him!"

As much as I may want to please my daughter, I don't try to pass. Reality has imposed its own demands. And I have to take the course my perception of that reality says is safe.

We all know how this principle works. We use it daily. We don't walk into walls — we look for doors. Walls are hard, and the way life is for us if we disregard reality and walk into a wall, we'll suffer a painful bruise. Our first learnings as children are like this. "Hot" takes on meaning when we discover the reality of burning pain, and from then on "hot" warns us not to touch. We've come to understand a little of reality, and we've learned to act accordingly.

In things like these the reality is easy to grasp. We can understand what life is like and act safely on our understanding. We learn to judge the distance of approaching cars; to walk where paths are clear; to avoid the pain of "hot" and "sharp." But in other things the reality is hard to see. Life as it is — "the way things are"; "what's best"; "what's real" — isn't easily perceived.

One of the most striking confrontations over just this issue took place in a Roman judgment hall in an old and dusty city. There were two men: one seated, free, with thousands ready to obey his command, the judge. The other stood bound, on trial, with hundreds outside shouting for his death. Still it was the judge who was nervous and uncertain, struggling to grasp the reality.

Jesus had been dragged before Pilate because the Jews were unable to impose the death penalty. That right the conquering Romans reserved to themselves. So now, after a night of illegal trial and hurried trips from one tribunal to another, a sleepless Jesus came before the man who claimed the power of life and death. Jesus was sent alone to an inner court where Pilate, after hearing the Jews' accusations outside on the steps, went back in to speak to Him.

"Are you the king of the Jews?"

"Are you asking me this of your own accord," replied Jesus, "or did other people speak to you about me?"

"Do you think *I* am a Jew?" replied Pilate. "It's your people and your chief priests who handed you over to me. What have you done, anyway?"

"My kingdom is not founded in this world — if it were, my servants would have fought to prevent my being handed over to the Jews. But in fact my kingdom is not founded on this at all."

"So you are a king, are you?" returned Pilate.

"Indeed I am a king," Jesus replied: "the reason for my birth and the reason for my coming into the world is to witness to the truth. Every man who loves truth recognizes my voice."

To which Pilate retorted, "What is 'truth?'" and went straight out to the Jews again . . .

(John 18:28f)

What Is Truth?

Pilate tried to sway the Jews, but they were determined. The hated Prophet must die. And Pilate, convinced of Jesus' innocence, was enough of a politician to realize that in this case it was best to give in. Still, what they said to him was disturbing: "he must die, for he made himself out to be Son of God!"

When Pilate heard them say this, he became much more uneasy and returned to the palace again and spoke to Jesus, "Where *do* you come from?"

But Jesus gave him no reply. So Pilate said to him: "Won't you speak to me? Don't you realize that I have the power to set you free, and I have the power to have you crucified?"

"You have no power at all against me," replied Jesus, "except what was given you from above. And for that reason the one who handed me over to you is even more guilty than you are."

From that moment Pilate tried hard to set him free, but the Jews were shouting: "If you set this man free, you are no friend of Caesar! Anyone who makes himself out to be a king is anti-Caesar!"

When Pilate heard this, he led Jesus outside and sat down upon the judgment seat in the place called the Pavement (in Hebrew, Gabbatha) . . . Pilate now said to the Jews, "Look, here is your king!"

At which they yelled, "Take him away, take him away, crucify him!"

"Am I to crucify your king?" Pilate asked them.

"Caesar is our king and no one else," replied the chief priests. And at this Pilate handed Jesus over to them for crucifixion.

(John 19:1f)

At first glance it seems easy to sketch the true situation. Here is a lone man, helpless before the hatred of His people, condemned by the man with power to free or crucify. Here is tragedy in the making: legal lynching. And the hopeless victim is utterly at the mercy of a vindictive mob and a vacillating ruler.

So it appears.

But the appearance is utterly deceiving!

The truth is that the lone man is in charge. "You have no power at all against me," is the reality. A victim, yes. Helpless and hopeless? Never! He is the Son of God, who *chooses* death — for you and me.

This is the truth. This is the reality.

Truth and reality are one.

Illusion and Reality

Reality is often hidden from us.

Illusion masquerades and blinds our senses so that what we perceive as true, as real, is utterly false.

And this, our difficulty in perceiving reality, is the real problem with views like those of Dr. Wolk. Lie to "cope with reality"? What *is* reality? How do we know that life as we see it isn't an illusion; that our assumptions about life are correct? Will a lie really preserve us from harm, or show love for others? Is life really like that — something we can manipulate with lies? Or is the idea that lies can make a positive contribution to the happiness of others merely an illusion; a shadow cast by warped perception? How do we know what life is *really* like?

So we are forced back to Pilate's question: "What is 'truth'?"

The Bible hints in many ways that one link in the chains that binds us is our blindness to reality. This blindness we think of as sight: a shimmering mirage that distorts and draws us toward emptiness. In Ephesians Paul calls this distorted idea of life "this world's ideas of living" (2:1f). John speaks bluntly of light and darkness, of walking in light and in dark, and warns that if we deny revealed reality we "live in a world of illusion and truth becomes a stranger to us" (1 John 1:5f).

Throughout the Bible "truth" and "reality" display an intimate connection. "Truth" in the Old and New Testaments, in the original languages, often reflects the concept of "in full harmony with reality"; "an accurate portrait of the way things really are." We can see this reflection clearly in the First John passage. Here we see God presented as Light, with no shadow of darkness existing in Him. The believer who enjoys fellowship with God cannot go on "living in darkness." To claim fellowship with such a God while we live in darkness would be both "telling and living a lie."

But what is "darkness"? Sin? No, not sin. Even in fellowship John says, we must still rely on the blood His Son shed to keep on cleansing us from all sin. John's talk of light and dark is not of sin, but of *living life as it is*. "If we refuse to admit we're sinners," he says, we live in that world of illusion and lose contact with truth. We must come to see ourselves as we are, and honestly face our helplessness. Failing to face the fact of sin keeps us struggling to perform, and forces us back under Law. And soon we lose our vision of the truth in bondage.

"But if we freely admit that we have sinned," the Word continues, "we find God utterly reliable and straightforward — he forgives our sins and makes us thoroughly clean from all that is evil. For if we take up the attitude 'we have not sinned' we flatly deny God's diagnosis of our condition and cut ourselves off from what he has to say to us" (1 John 1:5f).

"Darkness" then speaks of *denial of God's diagnosis* and *failure to live in accord with it*. "Light" is reality as known by God: "darkness" in the world of illusion. And to know reality as God knows it, to respond to life guided by His perceptions of what is real, is walking in the light.

It's clear when we think about it. Who can pierce through the illusions and mirages that distort our ideas of life? Only God. Who can *know* what's right and good: what harms us and others, and what shows love? Only God. Our motives may be good — but who has wisdom to transform an act of love into an act of intelligent love? Only God. *Not one of us, trapped as we are in our culture and our time and warped within by sin can say, "This is the way I have to behave to cope with reality!"*

Pilate's question, then, was hardly the sarcastic retort of a hardened skeptic. It was the sad reaction of a man who had struggled with life's meaning and found no way to know reality. Thus he reacted to One who claimed to have the Truth.

It is to this very point a Living Word speaks plainly to us. Jesus claimed to know the Truth. And Jesus taught that Truth was revealed in His words. His prayer for us takes on a special meaning: "Sanctify them [progressively transform and set them apart to Me] through thy Truth: Thy Word is Truth."

God alone has a vantage point from which to see reality. He alone is able to diagnose, to share an accurate perception of reality with us. He alone knows truth.

But now He has revealed it.

God's Word is Truth.

Till now I've spoken of Scripture as a Book of relationship: a Book revealing man and God, and calling us to growing trust in Him. And that it is. But often people who focus on relationship question the objective Word. They talk of "relational truth" while denying "propositional truth." God's Word *is* relational truth: every expression of the Word must be read through Christ; Christ alone gives meaning, and through Him the delicate hues of Love touch even the most difficult statement.

But every expression of the Word *should be read.*

"All are sinners" is reality in propositional form. The words say what they mean: their content is clear. And this true information is given us by God that we might know life as it is, and knowing reality find relationship with Him.

Unless we want to lose ourselves in darkness, we must accept the diagnosis of God's Word, accept the reality revealed, and pattern our lives fully on His Truth.

It shouldn't be hard to understand. God calls us to a relationship in which He shares Himself fully. He gives His love, and not His love only. He also shares His understanding of life. His insight into reality. His light.

And for a walk of fellowship with Him He calls us to walk in His light.

Christ reflects the same thing in His story of two home builders:

> Everyone who hears these words of mine and puts them into practice is like a sensible man who builds his house on the rock. Down came the rain and up came the floods, while the winds blew and roared upon that house — it did not fall because its foundations were on the rock. Everyone who hears these words of mine and does not follow them can be compared with a foolish man who built his house on the sand. Down came the rain and up came the floods, while the winds blew and battered that house till it collapsed, and fell with a great crash.
>
> (Matt. 7:24f)

God sees life as it really is.

He shares reality in the Word of God: a Word that is True because it accurately and fully expresses a reality we can experience.

For the Word to become a Living Word, we must learn to read its words as Truth.

Coping With Reality

There are many objections I might raise to Dr. Wolk's advice that we train our children to be liars. Avoid ego-damaging guilt? Doesn't guilt bring us to ourselves, and teach us to turn to Christ for forgiveness? When one of my children fights to hide guilt from himself I'm far more concerned. Tell lies to please others? How could they ever trust me for an honest word? Lie to avoid unpleasantness for me? Will this make me a stronger, more responsible person? And, perhaps most tragic of all, can a child trained to lie ever trust? Won't he be trapped in that awful gulf where we find ourselves cut off from others?

I could raise these objections, and others. But ultimately

I am forced back to one fact. Over and over again the Word of God speaks of lying, and *always* in tones like these: "Finish, then, with lying, and tell your neighbor the truth" (Eph. 4:17f). Lying is part of an old way of life and has no place in that "new life which was made by God's design for righteousness and the holiness which is no illusion."

Here I am forced to take a stand on one view of reality, or the other.

Today "situation ethics" appealing position demands that the only reality we recognize be that of "love." Like Dr. Wolk, men of this persuasion suggest that situations and circumstances govern how love be expressed. Lie? Surely, at times, if it's for the best. Old rules and blunt statements like "finish with lying" have no place in the reality they see.

But to whose reality am I to commit myself? Who knows what life is really like, and what in *this* reality best shows love?

For me there can be only one answer — Christ's. "Thy Word is Truth." If I were to leave the reality revealed by God so plainly in His Word, I'd stumble back into illusion. The transforming truth I need would become a stranger. And I'd lose my grasp on Scripture as a Living Word.

This is a thing no believer dare do if he yearns for transformation. The words of God are sanctifying Truth. They open up for us a vision of reality by which we are called to live. Suddenly the fog lifts; God's Word speaks out — "This is the way . . . walk in it!"

Walking in it, choosing to live life as God portrays it, I find transformation begun. I find a Living Word.

ADVENTURE

Seeing Scripture as Living Word forces our attention to our experiences in life. To study the Word together, we need to learn to share ourselves and our experiences with others, and to evaluate life by the reality the Word reveals.

This *Adventure* moves more deeply into both the sharing of experience, and the evaluation of life by the Word.

EXPLORATION 1

Share with the group an experience in which you resorted to a lie to "cope" with the realities as you saw and felt them.

EXPLORATION 2

Discuss the experiences you have just shared. How do you feel about them now — do you feel what you did helped, or hurt? Why?

EXPLORATION 3

In this section of the book, Scripture has been viewed as revealing God's perception of reality. Study Matthew 6 together, beginning at verse 19. What is being asserted about the way life really is? Express it in your own words.

EXPLORATION 4

Bring your own lives under the scrutiny of this Word. Share with others . . .

(1) Any principles revealed in Matthew 6 on which you have acted.

(2) Any situation you face now in which these principles seem to apply. What would you do if you were to choose to act according to the Word?

IN TRUTH

Principles

1. The Bible is given us for our transformation.
2. God *never* speaks to believers in tones of Law.
3. God's words are words of Gospel.
4. God never speaks or acts contrary to His love for us.
5. God's ability to express His love is unlimited.
6. God's Word reveals reality as He alone knows it.
7. God is an intervening, acting God.

7

Under Control

Often we feel that the life God's Word
describes is too much for us, too far
beyond us. But there's a special conviction
that frees us to trust and act on the picture
of reality the Bible reveals. And this is
a conviction about God; a perspective
on the kind of God He is.
God is an intervening, acting God.

There's something absurd in asserting that the world of
common sense is simply a grand impersonation of reality.
That the scene in Pilate's judgment hall where appearance
masks Truth so brilliantly, is constantly repeated in our own
daily lives.

But this is what we're driven to.

Somehow Scripture's portrait of life is far more real than
what we call "reality." Strip away the staging in the situation where in order to cope we lie; see the reality, and we'll
know that only honesty will do.

This conviction, this faith, lets us live by the foolishness
of God's Word. It lets us assert that "God has chosen what
the world calls foolish to shame the wise; . . . what the world
calls weak to shame the strong; . . . things of little strength
and small repute, yes, and even things which have no real
existence to explode the pretentions of the things that are"
(1 Cor. 1:26f).

Scripture turns our world upside down, and calls us to
live life responding to the beat of a distant, unheard drum.

None of this guarantees a "happier" life. Or promises that
judging situations by the Truth of Scripture will permit us to
escape from life. In fact, one of the absurdities of God's
Word is located exactly here. Reality calls on us to stop

the struggle to escape. Lie to "avoid unpleasantness?" No, be honest. And if we suffer for the truth, then well and good. Life's meaning isn't found in momentary pleasures or the absence of pain.

If we take Scripture seriously, we're forced to see even suffering and trial as bearing the potential for good. "When all kinds of trials and temptations crowd into your lives," the Bible says, "don't resist them as intruders, but welcome them as friends! Realize that they come to test your faith and to produce in you the quality of endurance. But let the process go on until that endurance is fully developed, and you will find you have become men of mature character with the right sort of independence" (James 1:2f). Relationship with Christ "means tremendous joy for you . . . even though at present you are temporarily harassed by all kinds of trials and temptations. This is no accident — it happens to prove your faith, which is infinitely more valuable than gold, and gold, even though it is ultimately perishable, must be purified by fire" (1 Peter 1:3f).

And thus the Bible turns life upside down.

Even tragedy is allowed to stand as the mark of God's transforming love.

No Accident

But let's not get the impression that the Christian life is one headlong rush toward misery. Instead, it's freedom to disregard appearances, and find life's meaning in living by God's Word. The reality Scripture reveals is marked out by this solid fact — God is in full control.

Submission to authority is one of those things that, like utter honesty, runs square against our grain. Today particularly it's popular to oppose — to buck the establishment, and strike out with any means at hand for what we call our "rights." This too is illusion. This idea that violation of our "rights" justifies violation of any law or rule. And it's a common illusion. We see it on the campus where destruction of property and disruption of classes is a common response to disliked policy. We see it on the streets, where policemen are coldly shot from ambush because they represent a system which is at times unjust. We see it in the anger of teens, and their frustration at parental rule. True, many parents aren't wise in their demands; some policies ought to be changed; injustice does exist. But do these faults justify our response? Is the best way, the right way, to rebel?

Many thoughtful and concerned people say yes. Without civil disobedience where would the black be today? Without a dramatic expression of concern, what board of regents would hear the student voice? And so the conviction grows in our society, the pattern of life is formed. Submit to authority? No, the way to cope in this harsh world is to rebel.

But Scripture brings us up short:

> Every Christian ought to submit to civil authorities, for all legitimate authority is derived from God's authority, and the existing authority is appointed under God. To oppose authority is to oppose God, and such opposition is bound to be punished.
> The honest citizen has no need to fear the keepers of law and order, but the dishonest man will always be nervous of them. If you want to avoid this anxiety just lead a law-abiding life, and all that can come your way is a word of approval.
>
> (Rom. 13:1f).

And this theme is expanded:

> Obey every man-made authority for the Lord's sake — whether it is the emperor, as the supreme ruler, or the governors whom he has appointed to punish evildoers and reward those who do good service. It is the will of God that you may thus silence the ill-informed criticisms of the foolish. . . . You who are servants should submit to your masters with proper respect — not only to the good and kind, but also to the difficult. A man does something valuable when he endures pain, as in the sight of God, though he knows he is suffering unjustly . . . In the same spirit you married women should adapt yourselves to your husbands, so that even if they do not obey the Word of God they may be won to God without a word being spoken, simply by seeing the pure and reverent behavior of you, their wives.
>
> (1 Peter 2:11f)

While not cutting us off from any legal redress, rebellion is condemned.

How can we accept this?

By realizing that Scripture·portrays reality. That appearances deceive. That what common sense shudders at and only faith accepts are in fact the principles on which this world runs.

This faith is reasonable, as God's Word explains. It's made reasonable by one fact: God controls. In First Peter, where submission is marked out as our way of life, Scripture strips away illusion with these words:

> He that will love life,
> And see good days,
> Let him refrain his tongue from evil,
> And his lips that they speak no guile;
> And let him (turn away) from evil, and do good;
> Let him seek peace and (pursue) it.
> For the eyes of the Lord are upon the righteous,
> And his ears are open to their supplication:
> But the face of the Lord is against them that do evil.
>
> (1 Peter 3:10-12)

The God we know as Lord is in control. He hears us: He has power to act. What happens to us when we choose the good is the careful decision of His will.

The passage goes on to explain that no one "in the ordinary way is likely to injure you for being enthusiastic for good." The normal course of man's life is smoothed, not made more dangerous, by acting against illusion and in accord with the reality God's Word describes. But, and here the original is graphic, "if it should happen, and it isn't likely" that a person suffers because he did the right thing, "that is a privilege. . . . concentrate on being completely devoted to Christ in your hearts . . . make sure that your conscience is perfectly clear . . . and *if it is the will of God that you should suffer* . . . fortify yourselves with that inner attitude Christ must have had" (1 Peter 3:8f).

The course of the argument is clear, and we are drawn back again to scenes of Calvary. Suffering that strikes us as a result of living in God's light is the direct result of God's own love-directed will. Like the tragic death of Christ, such little tragedies hold out the promise of a good that we may only guess at, until its results work out in life and beyond.

And so we're thrown back again on faith.

Faith, and God's assurance that "for those who love God, who are called according to his plan, everything that happens fits into a pattern for good" (Rom. 8:28).

God Himself is in control.

He oversees the outcome of each choice we make.

And, walking in the Light, we find His good.

Life As It Is

When we see the Bible as God's description of reality, life stripped of delusion and revealed to us as it is, Scripture becomes a new Book to us. We understand its saying from a new perspective.

Firstly it marks the death of our intellectualism, and the renewal of life. By this I mean we can no longer see God's Word primarily as information, as lists of things to learn. If it were just information, it might be all right for us to learn it. To master points of doctrine, and struggle to define our beliefs. It might be all right to put the Bible in a school, to hold classes, and give tests to see how much we can repeat. It might be all right (when we sit down together to look into the Word) to hold detached debates about ideas.

But the Bible wasn't given us to satisfy our curiosity. It is Truth and Light. It comes to us as a Living Word to illuminate life, and mark out for us the principles by which we are to live. "Live life, then," the Bible says, "with a due sense of responsibility, not as men who do not know the meaning and purpose of life but as *those who do* (Eph. 5: 15). And again, "brace up your minds, and, as men who know what they are doing, rest the full weight of your hopes on the grace that will be yours when Jesus Christ reveals himself. Live as obedient children before God" (1 Peter 1: 13f). When we come to the Word of God, then, we come to submit our every perception, our every experience, to its evaluation. When we sit down together to study the Word, we aren't gathered to debate ideas, but to share experiences, and learn to walk in Light. A Living Word can only be read as God's guide to life, that, *knowing what we are doing,* we might choose to live obediently.

This idea, that the Bible essentially is Light, helps us interpret it too. Not only are we warned away from sterile disputes and invited to explore experience, we have a striking guide to what the Word actually says. And when we measure some of our ideas about what the Bible teaches by this new understanding of the Word, we discover that much of what we think we've learned is wrong!

Some time ago I read a book on prayer that terrorized me. It took a number of familiar verses and constructed a set of "seven conditions" for getting answers to our prayers. If these conditions were fulfilled, the author said, prayer would be answered. Otherwise we had little hope.

The idea disturbed me, but as verse was piled on verse, I was convinced. The Bible *did* teach "conditions" for answered prayer. I could see no way out: "when you pray in faith, believing, you shall receive" . . . "when you ask anything in God's will. . . ." And my heart sank. I knew my prayers more often expressed doubt than faith, and then often revealed a dreadful uncertainty of His will. And I was trapped, cut off by obstacles I couldn't overcome.

But then the Word of God was seen as His revelation of reality . . . and all changed. The "conditions" took on new form, and I learned something of differences between "if . . . then's."

What differences? Let's see, by looking at two different situations. (1) In the first we see a mother watching TV. Her son comes in the door, and without taking her eyes off the set she warns, "If you walk in front of me and block my view, I'll club you!" A conditional statement has been made. (2) Another mother is cooking supper when her son comes in. She sees him look inquiringly toward the stove, and says, "If you touch that pot, you'll get burned." Again a conditional statement has been made — but what a difference!

The first we have to hear as a selfish demand is a coercive attempt to force the child to her will. The second we hear as love. It's the child's good the mother clearly has in view, and any harm that may come will be the natural consequence of disregarding a reality of which he's been made aware. There's no coercion here, or threat of force to make him act against his will. Instead each word is said to guide away from harm, and toward what is good.

To view the Bible's statements about prayer as "condi-

*tions" we must meet before God bends to answer is to im-
pose the character of that first mother on a God we know
is love.* God acts, but as the second mother He acts for
our good, and every word He speaks we can understand
just as we understand her words.

This is what I meant earlier when I suggested that "legalism" is rooted in us, not in the Word. Does God command?

Say "thou shalt not!"

"Thou shalt!"

"Love your neighbor."

"Lie not at all."

Certainly God commands. But only our failure to understand Him and His words permits us to see such words as
demand, as insistence that we perform.

Knowing God in Christ, knowing His Word as a revelation of the life that really is, we understand each word as
the guidance of a loving God, warning us away from harm.

And suddenly the sternness and the anger we once thought
we heard are gone. The coldness of a superior's command,
the *uncaringness* of words that insist we act against our will,
is gone. And in its place? The honest tones of love, opening up for us a life that's life indeed.

It's this way with prayer.

God hasn't spoken to restrict, to cut me off from Him, for
failure to perform. Seen now as love, speaking the message
of reality, "pray in faith, believing," is transformed. It stands
as promise. Promise of a reality to experience in Christ. It
tells of a time when, as we come to God in prayer, He
creates in us a faith that lets us know He has heard. And
that He will *do.*

There's much else we have to throw off, to relearn, when
we see God as Love and His Word as Light. How glad I
am to throw off all thought of "conditions" in my prayer.
To now "approach the throne of grace with fullest confidence, that we may receive mercy for our failures and grace
to help in the hour of need" (Heb. 4:14f).

This is life!

Life abandoned — to His love.

ADVENTURE

The difference between *invitation* and *command* is one
you need to explore with one another, through your own

experiences and Scripture. To help each other hear God's Word in tones of the second, not the first, mother.

EXPLORATION 1

Can you think of a time when you "suffered for doing right"? Share with the others, focusing on how you felt in the situation, and how you feel about it now.

EXPLORATION 2

Study together First John 1:1-10. How does the passage illuminate principles this book has suggested for discovery of a Living Word?

EXPLORATION 3

Study together First John 2:1-11. What perceptions of reality does God share here? Discuss.

(1)   Talk over with the others any experiences you've had in the past to which this understanding seems relevant.

(2)   Talk over any situations you face right now in which this reality seems to speak to you as God's guidance.

Principles

1.   The Bible is given us for our transformation.
2.   God *never* speaks to believers in tones of Law.
3.   God's words are words of Gospel.
4.   God never speaks or acts contrary to His love for us.
5.   God's ability to express His love is unlimited.
6.   God's Word reveals reality as He alone knows it.
7.   God is an intervening, acting God.
8.   The indwelling Christ enables us to experience reality.

8

New Life — Experienced

There are many ways in which Christ is the
message — and the key to understanding —
of the Bible. There is another way yet
not mentioned, a biblical perspective that
is utterly basic to every word God
speaks to us:
   **The indwelling Christ enables us to ex-
perience reality.**

Understanding Scripture as Truth, God's sketch of life
as it can become, brings a fresh excitement to the Word.
God's call to us promises renewal of life, and nothing less.
   The idea that Christian faith involves the call to *experience*
new life is reinforced constantly by the Word.

> Your goodness must be accompanied by knowledge, your
> knowledge by self-control, your self-control by the ability
> to endure. Your endurance too must always be accom-
> panied by devotion to God; that in turn must have in it
> the quality of brotherliness, and your brotherliness must
> lead on to Christian love. If you have these qualities ex-
> isting and growing in you then it means that knowing our
> Lord Jesus Christ has not made your lives either complacent
> or unproductive. The man whose life fails to exhibit these
> qualities is shortsighted — he can no longer see the reason
> why he was cleansed from his former sins.
> Set your minds, then, on endorsing by your conduct the
> fact that God has called and chosen you. . . .
>   (2 Peter 1:3f)

Jesus, too, insisted that men experience reality — faith
permits nothing less. We see it clearly in His discussion with
a man who, on hearing the story of the good Samaritan,
finally realized that each man is neighbor and that showing
practical sympathy is neighbor-love. Jesus wasn't satisfied
to bring him to this insight: His final words were "then you
go and do the same."

Much of Scripture's Good News involves revealing reality and calling us to taste it. There's a pattern for our lives set in the New Testament letters; a pattern that strikes a responsive chord in each of us. "Be calm, self-controlled men of prayer," the Bible says. And we want to. "Above everything else be sure that you have a real deep love for one another, remembering how love can 'cover a multitude of sins.' Be hospitable to one another without secretly wishing you hadn't got to be! Serve one another with the particular gifts God has given you . . . " (1 Peter 4:7f). And all this we want to do.

Something in us now is eager to respond.

But . . .

Realities Collide

She was a quiet girl, in her late twenties, dark hair framing a pale face, and very pretty. She'd been seated in back each Wednesday night of the meetings I'd held with the church.

The meetings had been frustrating for me. I was struggling with new ways of thinking about the church, and trying to persuade this congregation that they needed to rethink their way of life. Finally, on the last night, I tried dramatically to warn them of the emptiness to which I feared their traditionalism might condemn them.[1] I focused on one man in an attempt to shock them to my way of thinking. Jack had come to know Christ recently, and was vibrantly excited by his faith. Each time he came to the little church I'd seen him eager to share what had happened that week — to whom he'd spoken of Christ, how God had become more real to him. Sketching quickly what all knew of him and his unusual enthusiasm, I concluded my appeal: "How tragic if Jack loses his enthusiasm and his sense of Christ's reality — in his life with you."

It was a foolish thing to say — it didn't convince anyone; in fact it hardened them in their resistance. And I know it was resented. But on the way out she stopped me, this quiet girl. And with just that emptiness I'd prophesied for

[1] The Zondervan book, *A New Face for the Church*, expresses my developed thought about the church, and is designed to help local congregations evaluate their life as a church, and discover ways to seek God's guidance in renewal.

Jack she said, "It happened to me. I was like him . . . three years ago. But now. . . ."

And before I could speak, she had slipped out.

I couldn't help thinking of her as I wrote the first paragraphs of this chapter.

She knew the eagerness of which I wrote — at first. The promises of renewal were something she had heard in a living Word. But when she spoke to me the eagerness had been drowned in disappointment, and the promises now seemed cruel and mocking.

I'm afraid life is like this for many Christians. Empty of fulfillment. We make honest efforts to live the life God describes — we struggle to hang on to our enthusiasm, to reach out for the reality that draws us. But more and more it begins to seem like a dream. Soon exhortations like "Let it be your ambition to live at peace with all men and to achieve holiness" seem cruel. The more our ambition grows, the more distant the prospect seems!

It would be easy were we only called to "believe." But we're not. No nod of agreement with Scripture, not even a fierce orthodoxy, can satisfy God — or us. We can settle for nothing less than experiencing the Truth God's Word speaks out.

Why don't we experience it?

Why can't we?

Why doesn't relationship with Christ immediately tear away every barrier, and life become a constant joy?

Because, soon after we realize the awesome fact that we've been touched by a Living Word and called to life, two realities converge. *The reality of what abundant life is meant to be, dashed brutally against the reality of who we are.*

Each effort to achieve the life we're called to — of love and devotion and obedience and self-control — brings us to the brink of our own limitations. The more we try, the more we experience bondage. We may glimpse abundant life, but it seems distant. And we're overwhelmed by the awesome presence of our helplessness — stretching like some vast gulf that cuts us off from the life we dimly see and for which we deeply yearn.

Life, limited at every turn by helplessness, turns to ashes.

To many of us, who make an honest effort to live life as the Word describes it, this gulf becomes the central feature of our experience. We're constantly aware of our weakness. Our hope of renewal grows dim as failure after failure piles upon our consciousness, and over and over again we prove the truth of God's diagnosis of us as sinners. Sometimes in desperation we resort to self-deceit. We insist the life we know is wonderful, that Christ is real. But over and over again our lack of love and warmth betrays the hollowness of our pose. Or we may keep on struggling, reaching within again and again for strength to make another try. And life resolves itself for us into a series of ups and downs — of brave attempts and bitter failures.

Whatever course we take, we seem thrown back on ourselves.

In our struggle to experience new life we strike the reality of who we are.

It seems we're severed from the hope of life by all we are.

The Third Reality

In our attempts to experience reality it is disastrous to forget that Scripture deals with three realities, not two.

The first reality is who *we* are. We see ourselves in bondage, helpless, able to glimpse the stars but never able even to struggle up out of the pit in which our nature traps us.

The next is life, and what *it* is. We're stripped of our illusions, and introduced to a love and holiness that draw us, eager to experience what's revealed.

The third reality is Christ. He, not the other two, is the *focus* of the Living Word. He, not they, claims our attention. For in Christ the great gulf is bridged — in Christ we're lifted beyond ourselves and freed to experience Life.

Just how this is done is hard to say.

We can only know that it *is* done. "He has rescued us," the Bible says, "from all that is really evil and called us to a life of holiness" (2 Tim. 1:3f). Somehow in Christ's death and resurrection He so clasped us to Himself that His death is ours; His Life is ours too. At least, this is what the Bible says. "We have, as it were, shared his death." So "let us rise and live our new lives with him! Let us never forget that our old selves died with him on the cross that the tyranny of sin over us might be broken — for a dead man can safely be said to be immune to the power of sin. And if we were dead men with him we can believe that we shall also be men newly alive with him" (Rom. 6:1f).

Within the mystical dimensions of this Word is the key to experienced reality. We do not live — He lives in us. "The secret is simply this: Christ *in you!* Yes, Christ *in you* bringing with him the hope of all the glorious things to come!" (Col. 1:26f).

Whatever this may mean, men have claimed to experience it. "As far as the Law is concerned," Paul writes, "I may consider that I died on the cross with Christ. And my present life is not that of the old 'I,' but the living Christ within me. The bodily life I now live, I live by believing in the Son of God, who loved me and sacrificed himself for me" (Gal. 2:20f). Somehow the limitations and the bondage of the "old 'I' " (which are our constant burden) are sluffed off, and the believer steps out, confident that it's not he but Christ within who lives the newness he experiences.

We find echoes of this throughout the Word. "You, so to speak . . . shared in his death, and in him are sharing the miracle of rising again to a new life — and all this because you have faith in the tremendous power of God, who raised Christ from the dead" (Col. 2:11f). The new life described is the result of "living by the power of God" (2 Cor. 6:1f); each charge and challenge is made reasonable because we can "be strong — not in yourselves but in the Lord, in the power of his boundless resource" (Eph. 6: 10f).

Forced back on ourselves we wallow in helplessness, exposing the death that lives in our nature. But when death is fully exposed, an entirely new source of power is revealed — "the life of Jesus may be plainly seen in our mortal lives" (2 Cor. 4:7f).

Plain Fact

How can this be?

This mystical talk of union with Christ, of One living in us as the source of power for a life we can't otherwise experience, leaves me stunned and uncomprehending. I can't touch Him, no scalpel will expose His presence. And yet it's just this, Christ within, which the Living Word describes. I can see dimly why it would have to be like this. My failures convince me no one but God Himself can live in harmony with the Word. I can even nod when logic seems to insist that God alone can perfectly fulfill the perfection of His will. Put that way, who but Christ could lead the life to which I'm called? If I'm to know holiness of life, He *must* create in me what He calls me to.

But still the grand incomprehensibleness of it all looms up and strikes me dumb.

Christ, *in me?*

Christ Himself, to take control of hand and tongue, and use them as His own in living out His life through me? Who can understand it?

Or even try?

And yet just exactly this is called by Christ, not miracle, but *plain fact.* He said it that last fateful evening with His disciples. "I am the real vine," He began, and sketched a real picture of living union with Him that leaves no room for other source of life. "Just as the branch cannot bear any fruit unless it shares the life of the vine, so you cannot produce anything unless you go on growing in me. I am the Vine itself; you are the branches. It is the man who shares my life and whose life I share who proves fruitful. *For the plain fact is that apart from me you can do nothing at all"* (John 15:1f).

Committing ourselves totally to this plain fact — to this reality we cannot comprehend — opens up for us the experience of new life.

By Faith

In the first part of this chapter I tried to describe the dilemma of a believer who sees new life, and blindly stumbles out to grab hold of it. Words like "honest effort," "struggle," and "try" kept coming up — as they do in the descriptions many believers give of their Christian lives. These words reveal a tragic misconception: a retreat in relationship with God to a performance basis, and a denial of Grace.

It's hard to grasp, but perhaps we can see that even to speak of faith as "trying" turns attention on ourselves. It assumes, to some extent, that *we*, not Christ, are responsible for our lives. Turning back to ourselves for resources we taste only the first reality — our utter bondage. And the experience of abundant life escapes us.

The Living Word once and for all casts off *all* thought of performance, and fixes our attention on Christ. As Peter walked safely on the waves as long as his gaze was fixed on the Lord, only to sink when distracted, we are invited by the Word to keep our eyes on Christ. God's plan is to *impart* righteousness, not demand it. And this, the Bible says, is "a process begun and continued by" faith. So, the Scripture says, "the righteous shall live by faith" (Rom. 1:17f).

Earlier we looked at faith as trust, created in us. Far from calling attention to some capacity or ability we have (and some persons have more of than others), "faith" in Scripture calls attention to God. Faith is always faith *in* God; it has no independent existence.

Some time ago my children had a peculiar game: it consisted of clear plastic over a cardboard square enclosing metallic dust, and a magnet. For hours the kids would sit and, with the magnet shape and reshape that dust. They formed faces, little men, animals, all sorts of things. The dust responded to the magnet's pull.

Faith operates like this. It would be foolish to talk of the dust moving by "its magnetic power." The power rests in the magnet: the dust responds. It would be just as foolish to speak of "faith" as though its power rested in us: we respond. The power to change is God's.

Living by faith takes on this character: *we respond to God's call as to One who is utterly faithful.*

Here is "the new spiritual principle of life 'in' Christ Jesus that lifts me out of the old vicious circle of sin and death." Christ lives in me. His power frees. Turning away from every thought of strength in me, I'm no longer compelled to live "by the dictates of our sinful nature." Faith responds in trusting obedience "to the promptings of the Spirit" (Rom. 8:1f).

Here finally the broad outlines of two ways of life begin to emerge. In the first way of life, forgetting we are "but dust," we struggle to reform ourselves. We hear the Scriptures as if they said, "you ought to live this way"; "do this";

"be that." Hearing tones of Law we struggle exhaustingly to force our twisted personalities into the shape of love and holiness that we see. And just because we try, we fail.

We have deserted faith.

Faith's way is the way of life. Now we remember always who we are, and that God knows us. We expect nothing from ourselves, and know that He expects the same. We hear in Scripture no tones but of Love, and see reality unveiled. Increasingly the conviction grows that the love and holiness revealed are just what God intends to work in us. So we abandon ourselves and all attempts to do and be, and we face life confidently.

How do we live confidently? Where the Word says "Love . . ." we cry, "Lord, I cannot love. You love through me." *And knowing God is trustworthy,* we reach out to others, expecting Him to create love in us where there is not love, hoping against all hope, and looking only to Him.

We have discovered faith.

And through faith we experience new life.

ADVENTURE

The Christian meets life with a shout of joy — he does not shrink back in fear.

This freedom to live comes with relationship in Christ, and the realization that Christ lives within. Christ's presence gives us the ability to immerse ourselves in new experiences, to get in beyond our depth with others. We don't have to hang back. Trusting Christ we can *live* — by faith.

At the same time, all life is threatening. And new experiences challenge us, breaking into the familiar, comfortable ways of life and thought that insulate us from others. It takes a living faith to help us let go of the familiar, and to try the new. A faith that is focused in Christ — not ourselves.

This *Adventure* may help loosen our tight and frantic grip on habit, and relax us enough to let trust carry us beyond ourselves.

EXPLORATION 1

On page 84 the Christian experience of two persons, Jack and a young woman, are alluded to. To which of these two do you feel your Christian life has been most akin? Share your experience with the others.

EXPLORATION 2

Have you ever sensed that you were in a situation way beyond your ability or strength, and it suddenly seemed as though God just picked you up and carried you over? Share that experience with the others too.

EXPLORATION 3

Lean back, and imagine yourself living totally by faith (sort of like the experience you've just described). Be adventurous, but practical. That is, don't visualize yourself in eighteenth century Africa dodging spears — stick to familiar scenes that make up your daily life. But in these familiar situations, let yourself go.

When you've fancied some scene that, for you, seems to be "living by faith," tell it as a story to the rest of the group.

EXPLORATION 4

How likely is what you've just described to happen for you? Study individually Hebrews 11:1-29, and jot down at least five insights you received into the life of faith. Pool the insights with the others, and look again at the stories you've told.

EXPLORATION 5

Briefly state one thing for which you can trust God for this coming week, and pray for each other.

Principles

1. The Bible is given us for our transformation.
2. God *never* speaks to believers in tones of Law.
3. God's words are words of Gospel.
4. God never speaks or acts contrary to His love for us.
5. God's ability to express His love is unlimited.
6. God's Word reveals reality as He alone knows it.
7. God is an intervening, acting God.
8. The indwelling Christ enables us to experience reality.
9. God's Word reveals what *He* will do in us.

9
New Life — Expressed

If we read the Bible to find out what God
expects of us, we've fallen back into a
"Law" way of understanding Him. But
God's Word is "not Law." What does
reading Scripture as Gospel, grasping
hold of Christ as He has been seen in the
earlier chapters to be, mean to our study?
It means an entirely new perspective
on what is written. It means that:
God's Word reveals what He will do in us.

On the masthead of a famous newspaper is a phrase
snatched from Jesus' lips, naïvely taken to express the paper's
task: "You shall know the truth, and the truth will make
you free." It's naïve, not because what Jesus said is wrong,
but because the expression is so terribly misunderstood.

It was misunderstood by the men to whom He spoke it
as well.

The Pharisees, always suspicious of Him as a rival, a threat
to their entrenched power over the people, had plotted carefully to trap Him into an unpopular stand. When the plot
failed, as recorded in John 8, they confronted Him head on
in a daring attempt to discredit Him. But He turned aside
each challenge, not deftly, but with a blunt statement of
the Truth. He told them plainly who He was; He claimed
that only He could see reality: He confronted them with
the fact that they did not even know the God they claimed
to represent.

And then, in an aside to those who did believe in Him,
He said, "If you are faithful to what I have said, you are
truly my disciples. And you will know the truth and the
truth will set you free!"

The Pharisees reacted violently to this. "We've never
been slaves! How can you say, 'you will be set free'?"

And Jesus returned, "Every man who commits sin is a
slave." The Pharisees rejected every word.

The argument continued, and in its angry heat the two

simple statements Jesus spoke of truth and freedom were overlooked. Even today, distorted by what men read into them, the fantastic freedom offered is lost to view.

"You shall know the truth, and truth will set you free."

We can understand it now, remembering what we've seen in earlier chapters. Truth speaks of reality. Knowing encompasses the whole of life. Such knowing is no mere intellectual grasp. It's *experience:* to know by entering, heart and soul and mind, into life.

Experiencing the reality that God portrays in His Word is freedom.

Freedom to become.

If we have any doubt of this interpretation, the preceding words settle it. "If you are faithful to what I have said. . . ." Or, and the King James Version puts it, "If you keep my words. . . ." God's Word, His revelation of real life, is to be lived, not learned. Living His words we discover freedom.

This is the position to which faith brings us. We are ready at last to commit ourselves fully to the trustworthiness of God. We are willing to act on what His Word says, knowing we cannot live the life described, but trusting God to live that life through and in us. We are ready, sinners though we be, to experience freedom from sin's power.

The Shape of Freedom

"It isn't like I thought it would be," is a phrase I often hear from Christians. This is an honest complaint: the expression of a person who is puzzled by the Christian life. And it raises valid questions. "What should we expect as Christians?" "What does relationship with Christ hold for me?"

Often our expectations are completely unrealistic. We may think of the Christian life as one free from tension, disappointments, and trial. But life is still *life.* And life, in this world, is never free of strain. Even Christ, the Bible says, "learned obedience through the things which He suffered." And Paul, the great apostle of life in Christ, speaks of times when he is "completely overcome," the burden "more than we could bear" (2 Cor. 1:8f). Life brings suffering, and suffering is never unmixed joy.

Some have the idea that the vital Christian life is one of dramatic accomplishment for God. The missionary and the evangelist are idealized, and when in the daily humdrum no thousands hear of Christ through us, or our fumbling efforts to speak of Him are met with indifference, our faith is crushed. We read stories of the lives of others — and the feeling grows that somehow we must be second class Christians, cut off from the reality others know.

Sometimes uncertainty leads us to look for great experiences as evidence of relationship with God. We seek an "it," and when no sudden burst of emotion or unusual sign comes, doubt grows. Even if the sign seems to appear, the sign itself is likely to draw our attention. And we may slide into a way of life in which faith is centered, not in God, but in finding, over and over again, that sign.

All of these are symptoms of misunderstanding. Of failure to realize just how God's life is expressed through us. Misunderstanding of what God yearns to do in us.

To understand — to see the shape of freedom the Living Word proclaims — we must return to *becoming*.

God doesn't care what we *do for Him.*

God does care what we *are in Him.*

He calls us to know His Truth, and by experiencing His truth to transcend ourselves, and to become.

Becoming

Christ Himself is the shape of freedom.

He walked this earth, as sinful and distorted a place in His day as it is in ours, and He perfectly expressed God's nature. He was conformed, not to the illusory pattern of life in which men walk, but to God's will. His relationship with men expressed the love and compassion God feels for all. And He expressed love perfectly. Knowing reality, He avoided the errors into which sin leads us. He never tried to love with lies! He did the Father's will.

It's this, then, that is the shape of our freedom; the end of our becoming. The *Christian life is nothing more or less than Christ, still living, expressing love through us.*

We see this in so many ways. "I am giving you a new commandment," Jesus said the night He died. "Love one another. Just as I have loved you . . . " (John 13:33f). And that same night the Lord of Glory dropped on His knees and stooped to wash men's feet. "I have given you an example," He said, "so that you may do as I have done" (John 13:1f). "As children copy their fathers you, as God's children, are to copy him. Live your lives in love — the same sort of love which Christ gives us and which he perfectly expressed when he gave himself up for us in sacrifice to God" (Eph. 5:1f). And again, "Let Christ be your example as to what your attitude should be. For he, who had always been God by nature, did not cling to his prerogatives as God's equal, but stripped himself of all privilege by consenting to be a slave by nature and being born as mortal man. And having become man, he humbled himself by living a life of utter obedience, even to the extent of dying, *and the death he died was the death of a common criminal!*" (Phil. 2:5f).

No wonder Scripture says, "Live life with a due sense of responsibility, not as men who do not know the meaning and purpose of life but as *those who do*" (Eph. 5:15f). The life to which we are called is Jesus' life: God's purpose is to make us holy, and, we wonder at the thought, *form Christ in us!*

This is God's design, for every believer. In His purpose "Christ is all that matters, for Christ lives in them all" (Col. 3:11).

In this context we can begin to understand the stress placed in the Bible on behavior. And why such statements breathe freedom to us, not the bondage we knew under Law. Passages like this take on new meaning:

> As, therefore, God's picked representatives of a new humanity, purified and beloved of God himself, be merciful in action, kindly in heart, humble in mind. Accept life, and be most patient and tolerant with one another, always ready to forgive if you have a difference with anyone. Forgive as freely as the Lord has forgiven you. And, above all else, be truly loving, for love is the golden chain of all the virtues.
>
> Col. 3:12f

What meaning do we find in such exhortation now? This. First of all, we discover what we can expect in our Christian life. God doesn't call us all to do great things, or to experience miraculous signs. Or to live each moment with awareness of victorious joy that makes trials seem insignificant. He calls us to be merciful, kindly, humble. To accept life, to be patient and tolerant, to forgive and to love. *And the work of God in us is marked by creation of just these things.* He transforms. And His power in us "produces in human life fruit such as these: love, joy, peace, patience, kindness, generosity, fidelity, tolerance and self control" (Gal. 5:22). It is this that life in Christ holds out to us, as we respond in simple trust to Him. Christ lives His life within, and we are renewed.

Christ Himself is the second thing we learn in passages like this. Each word describes, not us, but Him. And this is what we need to see. We need to see how He intends to live within, so we can trust Him to recreate. Seeing Christ we realize such expressions have no hint of law. When the Bible speaks of life, the life we're called to live in Christ, Christ is revealed.

How then can we respond?

There is only one response to Christ so revealed: trust. "Trying" tied as it is to "ought" has no place here. *This is not what God expects of us: it is what God expects to do in us.*

When we realize this we can respond in simple trust.

Are we angry? Then we can abandon ourselves and all our efforts and can say to our enemy, "I forgive." Trust knows that Christ within will wash away the bitterness that's there, and flood our hearts with His forgiving love.

Are we proud? We can abandon ourselves and all our efforts to restrain our pride, and praise our rival. Trust knows that Christ within will, as we speak, replace our pride and create His humility within.

Do we lack love? Then we can abandon our shame and all our pretense and say, "I love you." Trust knows that Christ within will dissolve the hardness of our hearts and reach out through us with love of His own.

Trusting Christ within, we act.

And acting we come to *know* the truth.

At last we're free.

The Place We Take Our Stand

At the beginning of this book I said it would offer no new method of Bible study, and propose no simple steps for

Christians who have abandoned reading Scripture as too dull a chore. I suggested instead that it would concentrate on the rediscovery of the Bible as God's "living and active" Word.

To me this meant that our misunderstandings, the distortions caused by our human ways of viewing life, must be cleared away. It meant that if we could only learn to read the Bible through the message of the Gospel, a Living Word would appear.

So we started on the task of clearing away our old, worn-out ideas, and we began learning to look at the Bible's message solely from the viewpoint of the Gospel, rejecting every competing point of view.

The first fact of the Gospel we saw reflected in Scripture was its completely realistic view of man. There is no fuzzy hopefulness here; no half-hearted attempt to stir up to greater efforts at living good lives. We may tend to forget just who we are — God never does. In the Gospel God comes to us, and with total disregard of all performance on our part, extends forgiveness in Christ. And so does the Word. *Every word the Bible speaks is spoken with full awareness of the bondage in which we live.* God speaks in command, with "ought," only to those who persist in hiding their helplessness behind a mask. And Law's sole task is to crush us, not beneath it, but to remove every prop so that the full weight of our sin and shame drags us down, and we recognize our chains.

When we accept ourselves as God accepts us, as lost sinners who are still, amazingly, the objects of His love, Law never speaks to us again. Realizing the death sin has worked in us, we struggle no more.

We know that what God says to us is not, "You ought . . ." "You must . . ." or "Try. . . ."

The second fact of the Gospel that colors our understanding of Scripture is the heart of the God it reveals. We learn to see God, not as some reflection of ourselves, but as our reverse image! Where we love for gain, He loves at a loss. Where we manipulate and hide our motives, He enters the world in Christ to expose Himself fully to us. Where we are empty of power to change ourselves, His overflowing power not only raises Christ, but reaches out through Him to bring us life in our mortality. The cross that shows us the love of

God, and the empty tomb that shows His power, reveal a God beyond our imagining. A God who never says, "you try." His word to us is always, "I can."

The third fact of the Gospel that we saw is reality revealed. Cross and Resurrection strip away all illusions that blind us to the true source and seat of power, and show the fullness of God's control. Each word of Scripture unveils more, and brushes away our confused ponderings about life with a sharp, sure portrait of what is real. The Truth, the reality, the way our world is ordered, the principles of holiness by which God rules in life and death, are now made plain. We no longer need to wonder.

We have His Word and words to live by.

Last of all we've seen the Gospel's way of life: a unique blending of the three realities, that contradicts common sense and makes us gasp at the wisdom of God's plan.

We see helpless men infused with Christ . . .

We see character transformed . . .

We see God, expressing Himself as before in flesh and blood, and this time not in sinless flesh but by transforming our corruption.

And seeing all this, we bow before the God who speaks His Living Word to us, and in us.

It changes the way we read.

Now we come to Scripture, not to learn, but to live. And trusting God, responsive to His Word, we become.

What is it we become? What has that restless yearning in us always driven us to find? What promise does a Living Word, rightly read, hold out?

The promise is that you and I might be "an open letter about Christ," written "not with pen and ink, but with the Spirit of the living God." The promise is that this very message that we read (of love, power and reality) will be rewritten, "not in stone" but in the lives of living men (2 Cor. 3:1f).

ADVENTURE

Being a Christian in the deepest sense doesn't lift us out of our station in life, or transport us to some exotic circumstance. Life goes on — outwardly pretty much the same.

But actually life is meant to be *inwardly* different. We explore how in this *Adventure*.

EXPLORATION 1

Tell the others what you expected from life as a new Christian. What did you think your life would be like?

EXPLORATION 2

What were your ideas about the Christian life when you joined this study group?

EXPLORATION 3

What would you say *now* about what it means for us to be Christians? What insight you've gained during the weeks you've met together has been most helpful to you?

EXPLORATION 4

Study together First John 2:29 through chapter 3. Read through the perspective provided by the Gospel: how does this passage speak to you as Living Word? What faith-response does it call out from you?

Principles

Section 1.
1. Seek to live Scripture, not just learn about it.
Section 2.
    LIFE AT ISSUE: to go from life's concerns to find God's guidance in Scripture . . .
10. Define a shared *concern*.

Section Two:
DISCOVERY

I. Life at Issue

Life confronts each of us with a host of conflicting attitudes and values: with urgent demands to make uncertain choices. And life brings each of us joy and challenge, hurt and doubts. Often we sense a need for direction and understanding, or for healing — and often when our sense of need is dulled by the hurried pace of life we need these most of all.

It's easy to say that, for times like these, God is the answer — that God is never too involved in the affairs of His far-flung universe to bend to speak, personally, with the individual. But how does God affirm His love? How does He speak? How does He gently loosen the tangled strings of our lives and move to restore our freedom to love and to act?

The Christian is convinced that God speaks to us in His Word, that the Holy Spirit who inspired Scripture breathes His guidance into heart and mind today through what is written. But still we have the question, How do we hear God speak? How do we move from our particular concern and search through Scripture's library of sixty-six books to find the particular insight we need to understand, and understanding to respond to God's love and bring our lives into harmony with Him?

It's this problem we face in these next three chapters. In them we discover how to go from life's concern to the Word to seek God's viewpoint, and to reach out for His guiding hand.

10

Hidden Lives

*"I think it would be awfully interesting to
find out what the Bible says about. . . . "
Sometimes Bible study groups tend to
start out like this — as an exercise in
satisfying curiosity. Certainly the Bible
says a lot of interesting things — things
it's good to be curious about. And there's
nothing wrong with digging to find out
about them. But curiosity is best satisfied
alone. Studying the Bible with others
is for something else.*

The book of Job thrusts us into the experience of a man
with a problem he could not solve; a question he could not
answer. Job had always believed in God, and he had put
his faith to work successfully. His concern for the poor, his
honesty and his dedication are noted in Scripture, and God's
approval is recorded. "There is none like him on the earth,
a blameless and upright man, who fears God and turns away
from evil" (Job 1:8). But suddenly this good man's founda-
tions were shaken. In the space of a single hour, with events
and timing all testifying to a divine intervention, all his possessions were stripped away and his children were killed by
a tornado. Shortly after Job found himself in agony from
a plague of boils that covered his body.

In this tragedy Job was driven toward despair. His doubts
and uncertainty were magnified when three friends came
to comfort him, and stayed to dispute about the cause and
cure of Job's misfortune. All their ponderings led to only
one conclusion: God must be punishing Job for sin. Job,
then, through confession and repentance might apply to God
for mercy. But Job argued. He knew his own heart. He
had not knowingly sinned; thus he could not confess. If God
were punishing him for sin, God was acting unjustly.

Yet in all his anguished argument Job could present no
alternate explanation for his suffering. Job, bound by the
knowledge that he had not sinned, and trapped by the no-

tion that God only brings suffering into human life as punishment for sin, knew mental and emotional anguish that far outweighed the physical.

The book of Job traces the broadening of Job's understanding of God's ways with men, and ends with all goods restored and Job in deeper relationship with the Lord. But Job's experience highlights something beyond the meaning of suffering. It demonstrates the fact that *when life forces a concern upon us, that concern touches our whole being.* Job was not motivated by mere *curiosity* to search for a cause of suffering beyond sin. This was no intellectual exercise for him. A driving need had engulfed him; had forced him to grapple with life as a whole person. Job *felt.* Job sensed his need with every aspect of his person.

Few of us will have a concern as great as Job's when we come to share in God's Word with others. But though our motivation for searching out God's counsel may differ in degree, *our motivation should be the same in kind.* That is, the concerns we deal with should be *whole person* concerns. Concerns that involve our being — our feelings and attitudes and choices as well as minds. What we seek to understand should be something that is important to us as persons.

Self-revelation

It's hard for us to share our concerns as whole persons. Most of us are used to living largely hidden lives — telling more or less freely our thoughts and ideas, but holding back the feelings and concerns which fill us out and give us substance as persons. In a sense we present a two-dimensional silhouette to others; a caricature (usually flattering) of who and what we really are.

We have our reasons. Good ones. We've learned that many people don't want to know us. That many simply don't care about the burdens and needs, the joys and successes, that fill out our lives and make them whole and real. And then, we've found that some will use what we tell to hurt us — to ridicule, to gossip, to reject. It's a terrible risk to share feelings and attitudes and perceptions of life with others who might not care.

But if we're to study the Bible together (and do more than satisfy curiosity), we need to grow in our ability to share with one another. *Concerns,* as we've seen, touch the whole person — and unless we know one another as whole persons, we'll not tap concerns. To have the Bible speak to our lives, we must bring our lives to it, and submit them to Christ's authority.

While it's never easy to reveal ourselves to others, awareness of two great truths can help us begin.

First, the nature of our relationships in Christ. Barb spoke of it in the first chapter. "I do know that right now these people who are praying for me, supporting me, loving me are people whom I trust and love with my very being." What Barb experienced is the *reality* of the Body of Christ. The reality of being so linked with other Christians that we are *sure* of their unconditional acceptance, and that we accept them the same way. The Bible pictures this as having "the same care for one another. If one member suffers, all suffer together; if one member is honored, all rejoice together" (1 Cor. 12:25, 26). In this context of unity and love we are free to bear one another's burdens — and to bare our burdens to one another.

While the Body of Christ is a reality, and each group of believers God draws together has the potential for experiencing it, it's also true that we *grow* together. This kind of love doesn't just happen. It's created in us as we grow to know other believers as whole persons. And getting to know each other this way is a process; it happens over a period of time, through sharing. [This is one reason why I suggested in the introduction that your group work through *Discovering a Living Word* before tackling this section. *Discovering* is designed to help you discover one another as persons, and to help you reveal yourself progressively to one another without pressure and without haste.] If you've been together for some time, as friends in a church or neighborhood, you may already have tasted the reality of Christ's Body. If you have, you'll find sharing concerns a growing joy. But if you're new together, remember as you take the first tentative risks of self-exposure what it is you are reaching out toward — acceptance and support and love that are *really there.* For Christ's Body is a reality, a reality we are invited to experience with growing joy.

Second, the pattern of self-revelation set in Scripture. While this pattern shines through many places in the Word, David the Psalmist is perhaps our best example of living openly as a whole person (for His Psalms not only were addressed to God; they were recited as public property!). David is truly a three-dimensional man. Even the emotions and thoughts most of us tend to hide for fear of disapproval, David was willing to express. When discouraged this leader of men found freedom to sigh,

> I am utterly spent and crushed;
> I groan because of the tumult of
> my heart.
>
> (Psalm 38:8)

David had known God's blessing, but when God seemed slow to meet his needs David didn't hesitate to complain.

> I say to God, my rock;
> "Why hast thou forgotten me?
> Why go I mourning because of
> the oppression of the enemy?"
>
> (Psalm 42:9)

David spoke freely of his joys and credited God with his many accomplishments. But David didn't express only what might seem pious or hinted of success. David, who knew so much of trust in God and who exhorted others to trust, still knew fear. And what he experienced he expressed.

> My heart is in anguish within me,
> the terrors of death have fallen
> upon me.
> Fear and trembling come upon me,
> and horror overwhelms me.
> And I say, "O that I had wings like
> a dove
> I would fly away and be at rest;
> yea, I would wander afar,
> I would lodge in the wilderness."
>
> (Psalm 55:4-7)

What all this says to me is that God, who presents David as the man after His own heart, gives us in David a striking pattern to follow. In our relationship with God, and in our relationship with fellow Christians, there is no *need* for hypocrisy. For hypocrisy, at root, is fear that others cannot accept and love us as we are. The Gospel sets such fears to rest. Jesus loves us, and in His cross He invites us to come freely to Him. He receives us as we are, and with gentle application of His incomprehensible power works through His Word and through our brothers to remold our personalities until we reflect Him.

The Body of Christ is a reality we can experience, and learning to reveal ourselves honestly as whole persons is God's pathway to supportive love.

A Common Bond

As difficult as it may be to begin to share, it's tremendously rewarding. And in unexpected ways.

The other night a guest on a talk show was telling how he composes private tunes when lying in bed at night. My wife laughed half in surprise, and said, "Why, I do that, too! I thought I was the only one." And then our fourteen-year-old confessed that he too is a midnight musician, and often lying alone even orchestrates his tunes, imagining first one instrument and then another.

It happens when our hidden lives are revealed. We discover that things we thought were peculiar to us are common property with others. It's the same with our concerns. Our doubts; our desires; our determined attempts that end in failure; our yearnings for a fresh awareness of God; the temptations that drain us; the choices we're forced to make — all these we share with others. The Bible says, "No temptation has overtaken you that is not common to man" (1 Cor. 10:13). The impact of this is often lost as we stress the promise of strength and a way of escape that accompanies it. But this is important in its own right: *What happens to us is common to man.* Sharing human nature with others, and sharing the environment of earth, our hidden lives are much the same. Details may differ, but specifics resolve themselves into common issues. A young woman grows to adulthood filled with angry resentment against her mother. A businessman is bitter about his partner's misuse of authority. A wife resents her husband's thoughtlessness and apparent neglect. The common bond is clearly seen; the common concern, for Christian men and women, pressing. How do we deal with the resentment and bitterness

that exists (no matter how we reject them in our hearts)?
How do we deal with the strain that exists (no matter how
we try to hide it) between two people?

Somehow life has bound us all up in a common bundle —
and as we reveal ourselves to one another we begin to sense
our common bond.

One group of friends discovered a common bond by accident. They were having coffee at Jerry and Debbie's house
after Sunday evening service when Jerry shared a problem.
It came out suddenly and unexpectedly: "What do you do
when a Christian cheats you?"

Instead of jumping in with easy answers, the others waited
as Jerry went on. He told of a contract job he'd placed
for a Christian company, and then been flatly told by the
owner that he wouldn't pay the commission. "It's not so
much the commission," Jerry said, "even though $5,000 is
a lot of money to me. My lawyer wants me to take him to
court — says we have an airtight case. But I can't feel right
about it. Even though I know he has a reputation for sharp
practices. I don't think he ought to get away with it, but
. . . I just don't know what to do. It's a pretty rotten feeling."

Jerry's reflective sharing of his concern reminded Bev of
a recent experience of her own. "I think I know what you
mean," she began. "The other day Bobby came home from
school and he was all upset. He'd taken this test — he hadn't
prepared for it as he should — and got a low grade. Well,
he said he knew about as much as anybody else, but half
the kids in his class cheated and they got a lot better grades
than he did. Of course, I told him he'd done the right thing
not to cheat, but neither Tom nor I could help him much.
I mean, what can you say? Everybody seems to get away
with things these days. It isn't fair, but. . . ."

Then Marge's voice bit sharply and bitterly into the conversation. "Talk about fair! Herb, tell them what's happening to you."

You could see Herb wasn't happy with the drift of the conversation. "I'd rather not, Marge. There's no use talking
about it."

"Well, there's no use letting it fester inside, either."

"I'm all right, Marge. Let it alone."

Marge's voice softened. "Herb, it's not all right. You've

been upset for months now. You're tense and irritable and I think you're getting bitter, too. Not that I could blame you."

Tom spoke up in his quiet way. "It's all right if you want to talk about it, Herb."

"Tom, I don't know that there's anything to talk about. It's just that another guy got a promotion at work that I'd expected — that had been promised to me. I don't want to sound like one of those sour-grapes people. I . . . well, I tell myself I wouldn't mind if he was a better editor than I am. I hope I wouldn't, anyway. But he's not better. He's not nearly as good. And I'm pretty sure, from rumors I've heard and a few other things, that he didn't get the job on merit. I . . . I think he did sort of a hatchet job on me. Nothing I can pinpoint, but I catch some of the people looking at me strangely — and the boss isn't nearly as cordial — and. . . . Well, I'm to the place where my stomach actually acts up when I turn down Parkside to the plant. I'm irritable at home. I snap at Marge and the kids. I seem to have lost interest in things. I . . . I guess it's really gotten to me."

Interpreting Experience

That conversation at Jerry's was the start of something for the three couples. Too often such conversations, when they do take place, are merely frustrating interludes. People talk about their concerns, but the brief sharing doesn't lead to constructive action. And each individual sinks back into lonely uncertainty.

Lonely uncertainty is *not* God's purpose for us. He has provided, in His Word and His Body, a supportive fellowship of love within which we're to search for and respond to God's will. This is what Jerry and Debbie, Tom and Bev, and Herb and Marge found. They reached out to each other, and together turned to seek God's guidance in His Word.

The first step they took together after sharing was to *interpret their experiences.* Somehow the telling of Jerry's tale reminded Bev of the complaint their son Tommy brought home. And Marge sensed a relationship to the problem that had dominated Herb's life the past months. What was the link? What issue was common to all of them?

This happens in most sharing relationships. Someone shares, and in an attempt to test and confirm what was heard another person says, "Here's something that happened to me. Is this what you're talking about? Have we felt something in common here?" Each new experience shared in this spirit builds awareness that we are bound together by life, and that the concerns which grip us are held in common with others.

It took the folk at Jerry's house a while, but finally they talked through their experiences and agreed that they were most troubled by the apparent success of the "bad guy," while the same success seemed denied to them. The prosperity of the wicked galled them, and they knew again the feelings of the child who cries to his father, "But it's not fair!"

It was late when they reached this conclusion. So they decided to meet again the next week. In the meantime, each would dig into the Bible and see what insights he could gain. Next week they'd meet to share what they discovered.

FOLLOW THROUGH

1. *Individual before meeting:* If the idea of sharing and self-revelation troubles you, look at one of the following books: *Living on the Growing Edge* (Bruce Larson, Zondervan) or *How Do I Fit In?* (Larry Richards, Moody). And in the group, share only what seems comfortable to you.

2. *Individual before meeting:* complete the worksheet (next page) after reading quickly through chapter 18 of this book.
   When you meet: in place of the Bible study segment in the procedure you agreed upon, share the concerns recorded on your worksheet and illustrate them with personal experiences.

3. *When you meet:* after all have shared, spend whatever time it takes to select a concern you have in common and to define it (see *Interpreting experience,* p. 109). Try to agree on one which seems important to all of you (either selected from chapter 18 or growing out of your sharing time), and agree on how to state it. [The folks at Jerry's house finally came up with this: "What about the success of the 'bad guy' when the 'good guys' are

denied that same success?" They might have defined it better — but it gave them enough direction to get them started hunting].

Record your statement of your concern on the work-sheet(s).

WORKSHEET Chapter 10

IN PREPARATION

1. Some thing(s) of concern to me from chapter 18 or personal experience is:

   _____

   _____

   _____

   _____

2. I can help the others understand this concern by sharing the following (experiences, incidents, feelings):

   _____

   _____

   _____

   _____

   _____

   _____

   _____

   _____

IN THE GROUP

3. After sharing, we agreed to concentrate on the following issue that's of concern to us all:

   _____

   _____

   _____

   _____

4. During the week I'd like to pray especially about:

   _____

   _____

   _____

   _____

Principles

Section 1.

Seek to live Scripture, not just learn about it.

Section 2.

LIFE AT ISSUE: to go from life's concerns to find God's guidance in Scripture . . .

10. Define a shared *concern*.
11. Search for *several* relevant Scripture *passages*.

11
By Searching

"Well I think. . . . " Funny how often that
phrase precedes some judgment only
God should be allowed to make. "I think
you ought to. . . . "; "I don't believe God
would expect. . . . "; "I suppose God
must. . . . "
 If we really do have in Scripture an
objective revelation of God's thoughts, His
purposes, and His patterns of working
in human life, how much better to search
out what God says rather than rely on
our own inadequate views of life.

Before the group at Jerry's house broke up, after they
had clearly stated their concern, they made one other important decision. They agreed to look for *passages* of Scripture that shed light on their problems.

It's true that often a single verse or even phrase gives
us an insight we've been seeking. For Martin Luther, Romans 1:17, "the just shall live by faith," burned bright and
shone out from the page, changing his life and, through him,
the course of history. *But Luther's doctrine wasn't based on
that verse alone.* The verse served as a personal catalyst;
and throughout his ministry Luther went to the major passages of Scripture to teach justification by faith in the context of the whole counsel of God.

This is what we need to search for when gripped by one
of life's concerns: the whole counsel of God. What pattern,
what broad perspective, what encompassing picture of reality does Scripture provide? For such an overall grasp of
truth, it's important to base our understanding on *passages,*
not phrases.

It's not hard to see why. Except for Proverbs, which is
by nature a collection of short, pithy generalizations, most
of Scripture contains *developed* thoughts. That is, paragraphs, sections of several chapters length, and often whole
books deal with a particular issue in its historical situation,
and present a developed argument.

For instance, the book of Job, which we mentioned last chapter, has a distinct development that helps us to understand its overall impact — and helps us interpret verses and paragraphs within it. Let's see how this works.

Outline of Job

PASSAGE	DEVELOPMENT
Job 1:1 - 2:10	Gives the background of Job's experience: Satan's challenge to test Job — which test Job passed (cf. 1:11; 2:5; 2:10).
Job 2:11 - 31:40	Job and his three friends debate the cause of his suffering. Through several rounds of dialog no one can suggest any cause but sin — though Job continues to state his innocence.
Job 32:1 - 37:24	Elihu, an observer of the dialog, breaks the impasse by demonstrating other purposes God may have for allowing suffering than as punishment for sin.
Job 38:1 - 42:32	God speaks to Job from a whirlwind; contrasts His power and wisdom with Job's limited understanding and ability.
Job 42:1-16	Job, now knowing God firsthand, submits fully to Him and His purposes; all he has lost is restored double.

The whole book of Job, then, fits together as a whole; a unified development of thought that links, and helps us understand, each part. Because the book is a whole, we would be *wrong to snatch a single paragraph out of the context and interpret it as though it stood alone.*

For instance, in one place the anguished Job cries out,

> But he is unchangeable and who can turn him?
> What he desires, that he does.
> For he will complete what he appoints for me;
> and many such things are in his mind.
> Therefore I am terrified at his presence;
> when I consider, I am in dread of him.
>
> (Job 23:13-15)

Is this an accurate portrait of God? Should our thoughts about Him, our feelings, be those of Job? After all, what Job says *is* in the Bible. So isn't it accurate?

The answer to such a question is, of course, found by putting these verses in their context in the book. Inspiration guarantees that Scripture accurately records Job's words, as God intended us to have them. Knowing the context, the place the verses have in the book's development, we can understand them for what they are; the anguished cry of a man who believes so completely in God that He is thrown into utter agony when that God acts in ways he cannot understand or reconcile. And tracing the book to its conclusion, we discover that Job's terror melts when he comes to know God better, and learns fully to trust His decisions.

The same point can be illustrated from chapters of books and sections within chapters. But perhaps the point has been made. In searching for God's perspective on life, it's best to look for *passages* where that perspective is *developed* — and not to base our understanding on a snatch of verse here or a phrase there. The Bible is written largely in *developed units of thought:* it's these blocks of developed thought that we need to look for.

So the decision made at Jerry's house was an important one. "We'll look for *passages* of Scripture that shed light on our problem."

Avenues to Discovery

How do we go about finding such passages? What approaches are open to us? There are many avenues we can take to lead us to exciting discoveries, and each member of the group at Jerry's took a different one.

Work from basic knowledge. Tom had spent a couple of years in Bible Institute, and had a pretty good working knowledge of Scripture. The more he thought about the group's discussion the first busy days of the next week, the more troubled he was about one thing. The group had defined the issue in terms of the "success" denied the "good guys." Was this the right way to look at it? Wasn't being under pressure, and even suffering, sometimes of greater benefit for the Christian than "success"? Maybe what they'd been looking at as *bad* was really *good!*

Using his working knowledge of the Bible,[1] Tom began to run down passages that talked about the role of pressure and suffering in the Christian's life.

Tom turned to several New Testament passages (the part of the Bible he knew best), and jotted down a number of notes on what he read. Here's one of the passages he found, and the kind of thing Tom felt was important to record (see Figure 3).

James 1:2-18

— *Various trials are an occasion for joy (v. 2)?*
Why?
They test faith (like, proving its strength) (v. 3),
"road-testing" cars?
The product is steadfastness (stability) and ultimately
maturity. (v. 4)
(maturity's worth a lot to me!)

— *We can expect God to give us wisdom (how to knowl-*
edge rather than information!) when we're in a bind
(v. 5), as long as we keep our trust focused in Him
(v. 6).

— *The real problem with testing and temptation isn't*
outside; it's inside us (v. 12-15). God doesn't put us
in spots to force us to sin — wrong responses to things
come from our inner desires — our inner natures.
(Maybe the big problem then is our upset when some-
thing unfair happens.) Back to that "joy" response
again. (v. 2)

Man, that's asking a lot!

Figure 3
Tom's notes on James 1:2-18

Tom was busy that week, and found only two other passages beside James 1; Hebrews 12:1-17, and 1 Peter 1:3-9.

---

[1] Chapters 13, 14, 15 show you how to start with Scripture and go on to build *your* working knowledge of the Word.

But he spent time thinking about each, and jotting down ideas to share when the group met the next Sunday.

Search for parallel experiences. Jerry and Debbie both had gone to Sunday school as children, and still went to church regularly. But they'd never really gotten into the Bible for themselves. Still, as they talked the problem over that Sunday night after they'd gone to bed, both thought of David, the Shepherd King. Somehow it seemed to both of them that David would have known how they felt — he'd had problems like theirs. So they decided to read in David's Psalms that week to see if they could gain insight from him.

Jerry and Debbie didn't approach the Bible systematically, but they had hit on one of the most profitable ways of moving from life concerns to Scripture.

I noted in the last chapter that our humanness, our sharing of earth's environment (with sin's warping of every society), unites us with others in a common bundle of shared life. We share life not only with those of our generation, but with those who have gone before. The experiences of men throughout the ages mirror our experiences, and the issues of life that demanded their attention are the same issues that demand ours. And so the Bible, looking back across the history of God's people, declares, "These things happened to them [in their historical situation] as a warning, *but they were written down for our instruction*" (1 Cor. 10: 12). In deciding to focus their search on the life of a man who had experiences that paralleled their own, Jerry and Debbie had fallen unaware on a basic method of Bible study.

It was an exciting week for the two of them, as many thoughts and feelings expressed in Psalms caught and reflected their concern. But the most exciting time came when they discovered Psalm 73, and read:

> But as for me, my feet had almost
> stumbled,
> my steps had well nigh slipped.
> For I was envious of the arrogant,
> when I saw the prosperity of
> the wicked.
> (Psalm 73:2, 3)

As they studied the Psalm together, they made notes too. Their method was a little different than Tom's. They jotted down snatches of the Psalm itself instead of summarizing what it said, and added their thoughts in a column beside what they recorded (see Figure 4).

Psalm 73	
v. 3 envious of arrogant . . . when saw prosperity	is that's what eating at us? envy?
v. 5 they are not in trouble	why don't they have problems like we do? they sure do seem to get away with it.
v. 10 so people turn & praise them	why does God let them get away with it? They do lead others to follow their example.
v. 11 they say "How can God know?"	Is their view of God best? He sure doesn't seem to act very fast!
v. 13 All in vain have I kept my heart clean.	Sometimes it sure does seem a waste of time to try and do right. Why doesn't it pay off? What's the good of it, anyway?
v. 17 went into Sanctuary of God . . . then I perceived their end	Guess we do have to evaluate in terms of eternity as well as time. How much of our upset comes from caring too much about things that aren't important?
v. 18 Truly thou (God) doest set them in slippery places	Success dangerous? Never tho't of it that way, but it's true. Maybe we've been getting on too well as it is. Is God reminding us of Him by this trouble? Of our values?

Figure 4
Jerry and Debbie's notes on Psalm 73

They talked about it a great deal that week, and when the next meeting came, Jerry and Debbie were ready.

Trace key words and ideas. Herb had a large concordance around the house someplace, so he dug it up and decided to try to find a helpful passage by looking up key words. The problem was, what words would he look up?

Looking over the issue as his group had stated it [What about the success of the "bad guys" when the "good guys" are denied that same success], he thought of some possibilities. First he tried "success," but found that the Bible just didn't use that word the way we do. It wasn't there! [If Herb had looked for a parallel term, he might have used "prosperity." He'd have found many entries. But he didn't think of it.] Herb did know that "good guy" and "bad guy" weren't exactly biblical terms either! But he knew biblical parallels for them — "righteous" and "wicked."

A look in the concordance showed dozens of "wickeds" and "righteouses' " scattered through the Bible. So Herb decided to look for places where they appeared *together*. It was a good idea. It not only shortened his hunt; it led him directly to places where the Bible compares and contrasts the patterns of life of the two.

In particular, it led him to two verses in Habakkuk (a book Herb couldn't remember having read).

> For the wicked surround the righteous,
>   so justice goes forth perverted. (1:4)
> Why dost thou look on faithless men
>   and art silent when the wicked
>   swallows up
>   the man more righteous than he? (1:13)

This last verse particularly gripped him. Addressed to God, it contained just the query he and his friends were grappling with! Through tracing key words in a concordance, Herb had discovered a whole book of Scripture that dealt directly with his concern.

It was hard to understand everything the writer was talking about, but as Herb read the short book over several times, the main outlines seemed to come clear. So he too jotted down his discoveries (Figure 5, p. 120).

The main thing Herb gained from his study was the clear impression that even while the sinner seems to be enjoying his greatest success, God is working inside his personality, and in circumstances, to judge him. That first part of chapter two really excited him. "The arrogant . . . will never have enough." Wow! No matter what success a person appears to have, when he gains it the wrong way or for the wrong motives, there's a growing emptiness inside that success can't fill. He'll never get *satisfaction* from his success!

HABAKKUK

1. asks God about permitting injustice in Israel *(1:1-4)*

2. God says He's planning to punish His people's sin using an enemy nation *(1:5-11)*

3. Habakkuk understands chastizing — but can't see how God can use a "big" sinner to punish a "little" sinner *(1:12-17)*

4. God seems to be telling Habakkuk that the sinner never really gets away with anything. Any sinner *(2:1-20)*

   Why?

   a. The arrogant never has enough (he can never find satisfaction!) *(2:1-6)*

   b. Others are going to pay him back — his actions give them scores to settle! *(2:7-8)*

   c. He can never be really secure. His way of life keeps him in danger *(2:9-11)*

   d. Only good is going to last — sin and its works will be destroyed in the end *(2:12-14)*

   e. (don't understand this one) *(2:15-17)*

   f. trusting false gods is useless — only God is alive and able to act *(2:18-19)*

5. Don't really understand chapter 3. Have to look it up somewhere later.

Figure 5
Herb's discoveries in Habakkuk

It was a lot to think about. And when the next meeting came, Herb was prepared to share.

Formulate hypothetical solutions. Marge was one of those people who operates on hunches. The more she thought about the problems she and her friends had, the more she felt the devil must have something to do with it. It seemed likely that Satan would want to keep his people satisfied, and so give them success, and at the same time want to make things so tough for Christians that they'd be tempted to give up on God. So Marge rummaged around in the Bible that week to see if she could prove her point.

It's dangerous, of course, to use the Bible to "prove your point." When you do, you shut your eyes to fresh ideas, and you may even misinterpret biblical evidence in your desire for support. It's best to go to Scripture to *learn;* not to prove what you think you already know.

But actually none of us comes to the Bible with mind wiped clear. We all bring whole sets of ideas, ways of thinking, categories. Marge did do one good thing — she made her presuppositions *explicit.* She said what she expected to find quite clearly: "perhaps Satan is behind our experiences and trying to use them."

Marge could have done even better if she'd jotted down additional hypotheses to check out. An obvious alternate idea, that would have opened up new avenues of research, is this: "Perhaps *God* is behind our experiences and trying to use them."

So it is helpful, in going from a life concern to Scripture, to think of *a number of possible solutions* to the problem posed. When these are stated, they'll open up avenues for search — and for discovery.

Marge looked up verses on Satan during the week. She didn't locate any major passage. But she came up with some things that seemed to fit in. She found Satan had a role in Job's suffering, and in Paul's "thorn in the flesh" (1 Cor. 12:7f). She read about the temptation of Jesus in Luke 4, and found a warning in First Peter 5 that did seem to tie Satan and suffering together. At least they were mentioned just a few verses apart.

Her thoughts were still disorganized. But when the next meeting came, she did have something to share.

Use topical tools. Bev took a shortcut in study that's often helpful, though at times there's a danger of violating a basic study principle — that of looking for *passages* rather than snatches of ideas. Bev went to her church library and asked for something that would help her. She was given *The Zondervan Topical Bible,* a book that gathers verses and paragraphs from all parts of Scripture and records the texts under topical headings. While it's important to remember the need to study the context of each verse and paragraph before we try interpreting Scripture, this book helped Bev locate some of the same passages the others had found — and quickly.

Other topical tools help too. References are printed in the margins of many Bibles which point to parallel passages. (Figure 6). The *Thompson Chain Reference Bible* follows topics through Scripture, beginning with a subject's first mention and attempting to lead to every mention of it on through the whole Book. These tools are aids to study. Like a concordance they may help us locate information that may otherwise be hidden from us.

12.20 2 Cor 2.1–4; 1 Cor 1.11; 3.3	20 For I fear that perhaps wish, and that you may fin there may be quarreling,
12.21 2 Cor 2.1,4; 13.2; Gal 5.19	gossip, conceit, and disorde God may humble me befor many of those who sinned impurity, immorality, and ticed.
13.1 2 Cor 12.14; Deut 19.15; Mt 18.16	13 This is the third time be sustained by the e· warned those who sinned l
13.3 Mt 10.20; 1 Cor 5.4; 2 Cor 9.8; 10.4	them now while absent, as I that if I come again I will no that Christ is speaking in m but is powerful in you. 4 F
13.4 Phil 2.7,8; 1 Pet 3.18; Rom 6.4,8; ver 9	lives by the power of God. I with you we shall live with l 5 Examine yourselves, to

Figure 6

Because each of the people who had shared his concern that first Sunday night felt a responsibility to the others, and felt a personal need for God's guidance, each was prepared when they met again. Each had something to share that he had gained in personal study of God's Word.

FOLLOW THROUGH

1. *Individual before meeting:* look through the avenues of approach to Scripture discussed in this chapter, paying particular attention to the charts showing how approaches can be used. Then fill out the worksheet on

the following pages, *working on the concern your group chose to explore at your last meeting.*

2. *Individual before meeting:* select *one* of the avenues of approach on which you've done preliminary work, and follow it into Scripture to gather information. Remember to look for *passages* that seem relevant to your topic rather than for single verses or phrases.

3. **When you meet,** share with the group what you've discovered in your Bible study, and jot down notes on passages and ideas they've discovered.

WORKSHEET Chapter 11

IN PREPARATION

1. Record your group's concern from the end of chapter 10.

   _____

   _____

2. Do *preliminary* work on each avenue of discovery for *your* concern.

   A. *Working from basic knowledge:*
   Do I know any passages which relate to this concern? What are they?

   _____

   _____

   B. *Searching for parallel experiences:*
   Do I know any Bible characters who had experiences such as the ones we talked about? Who are they?

   _____

   _____

   C. *Tracing key words and ideas:*
   What key words might, if traced through a concordance, lead me to relevant biblical passages? Words about ideas? Feelings? Which would be worth checking out?

   _____

   _____

   _____

D. *Formulating hypothetical solutions:*
What possible results might I expect to get from my study? Can I list several alternate, possible learnings from the study?

_____

_____

E. *Using topical tools:*
What topics might I look up in a tool such as a topical Bible or chain reference Bible?

_____

_____

3. Choose one of the five avenues on which you've done preliminary work and follow it through as outlined in the chapter, to gather information on your concern. Record your findings on a separate sheet(s) of paper.

IN THE GROUP

4. Record here passages and insights that others in your group have to share from their preparatory Bible study.

_____

_____

_____

_____

_____

_____

Principles

Section 1.

Seek to live Scripture, not just learn about it.
Section 2.

LIFE AT ISSUE: to go from life's concerns to find God's guidance in Scripture . . .

10. Define a shared *concern.*
11. Search for *several* relevant Scripture *passages.*
12. Let the *biblical perspective* guide your *response.*

12
Portraying Reality

"But this verse leads me to. . . . " We
mentioned it before. A Bible verse or phrase
may, and often does, serve as a personal catalyst to open our eyes to exciting,
even life-changing Truth. But it's important to build our understanding of life,
and to commit ourselves to action, on
something more substantial. Really, we
need a broad picture of life as seen
from God's perspective. We need to understand revealed reality.

One of the ways our minds work is by putting things together. By interrelating. The paperback detective story
builds on this, and throws out a host of clues and false clues,
challenging us to link them all together to solve the crime
the author has described. Most of us rather enjoy the challenge.

But what's entertaining in paperback is often grim in life.
For everyday life challenges us too — and hurts us when
we come to the wrong solutions. Misreading the clues and
seeing a wrong pattern in life can lead to tragically wrong
decisions.

We really do need to see patterns to interpret situational
clues correctly. A traffic system has a pattern, and it works
because all drivers understand traffic clues the same way.
The light turns red; all stop. Green; all go. We slow for
45-mile-an-hour signs; look both ways when approaching
a yellow upside-down triangle that says "Yield"; and we
know what a flashing light on one side of the car in front
of us means. We pull over when an ambulance or police
siren sounds behind us, and pull up to a four-way Stop sign.
And we wait our turn at the Stop sign — or risk the angry
looks of others who expected us to take our turn.

A traffic system works because we all perceive these signs
and clues to action in the same way. We understand them,
we respond to them, we know the pattern. But if we re-

spond wrongly, we risk the penalty of a ticket — or the tragic rending of metal and flesh that marks an accident.

The pattern isn't as clearly marked out for most of life. There are signposts, clues that circumstances and other persons give us. But in our world today there's much disagreement as to what each means, and how we should respond.

It was this uncertainty about the meaning of their experiences, about how they should be understood and how believers should respond, that had drawn Jerry and Debbie, Tom and Bev, and Herb and Marge together. It was the need to see a pattern in life, and seeking the pattern to be guided to make good decisions, that had led them to Scripture. They wanted an interpreting Word from God.

Whose Worldview?

The standpoint from which any of us perceives life, his presuppositions about it, is the framework of his *worldview.* Choices, and the experiences they lead to; values and priorities; feelings and attitudes — all fill out the framework and grow into the unique, yet common-to-man way one perceives life. Thus our worldview is the perspective from which we evaluate each experience and respond to each situation.

It's tragically clear from human history, from the pages of our daily newspapers, and from personal choices which have hurt us and others, that every person's worldview is inadequate. It does not reveal reality adequately. It leaves us uncertain and groping at many points.

The Bible reveals the reason for our failure. Because of sin human beings are condemned to "drift along on this world's ideas of living," and are trapped in a world of "illusion" (Eph. 2:1-5). Sin's force has not only twisted the will so that we choose wrong willfully, it has also warped human ability to evaluate life accurately. We see illusions, we look on life with a distorted perspective. And our failure to understand is often responsible for disastrous decisions.

Not being able to trust our own perception of life, we are driven to seek God's. Our only hope is to pierce through to reality, to the true pattern of life, by discovering — and learning to live by — God's worldview.

Excitingly, this is possible for the Christian! The new life

God gives us in Christ creates in us a capacity for accurate perception. As Scripture says, "we have the mind of Christ" (1 Cor. 2:16). Our potential for understanding comes first of all from the Holy Spirit, who settles down into the life of the believer to guide him. And second, our potential comes from the Scripture, which is the *objective revelation* of God's viewpoint. We reach out for reality by coming to the Word of God to discover God's worldview, relying on the Holy Spirit to guide our understanding and our response.

It's important to remember that what we seek in Scripture is a worldview — a patterned perspective on life. The traffic signs I just referred to are meaningful *within the traffic system.* Because each is part of a unified whole, each can be understood in relationship to the whole. *When we come to the Bible for answers to life concerns, we're not seeking a single sign or clue. We're looking for a pattern. We're looking for a perspective on life from which to interpret and understand the situations in which we find ourselves.*

When the three couples got together at Jerry's the next week, each had information to share. They had discovered a variety of clues. Fit together in a pattern, these could give a broader understanding of reality — could show how God works in time and in eternity.

Let's review some of the information the six had gathered in their personal Bible study:

1. God Himself uses trials for our good.
2. Trials can help us toward maturity.
3. God promises us wisdom for making right choices in trials.
4. We have to consider the end of saint and sinner when evaluating "success." No one "gets away with it."
5. Success can be a dangerous thing.
6. We have to watch out for envy of the successful bad guy.
7. Sometimes the wicked seem to win out on this earth.
8. But the successful wicked aren't really happy — they can never be *satisfied.*
9. There's no security in grabbing for things the wrong way — you get enemies who will be out to get you.
10. Pinning life on "success" is like trusting in an unreal, false God.
11. Etc.

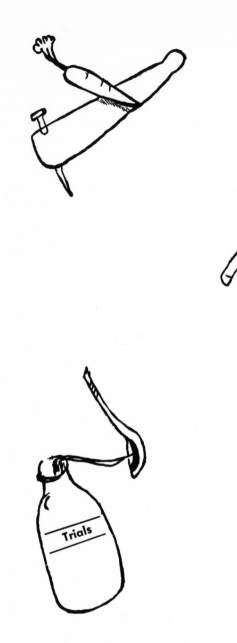

"Richard Cory" Syndrome

Figure 7

How could the couples put these together to help them see the pattern, the "portrait of reality" that Scripture presents? They decided to try to visualize. Actually to sketch a portrait of revealed reality (see Figure 7).

How could they show the main features? It was rather fun — and sometimes funny — to decide what to sketch. Someone suggested that Psalm 73, with its stress on evaluating the wicked and righteous ways by their ends, was something like a carrot and stick combination. The carrot (reward) was out ahead to motivate, and the stick (punishment) was there too. A guy could take his choice. It was a little crude but they drew it in at the far right.

When they were talking about trials being good for you, Marge thought of some bad tasting medicine her grandmother had given her. No matter how she complained, grandma insisted, "But it's good for you!"

"I couldn't see it then," Marge said, "but I did get better. Maybe it really did help."

So they represented trying times for believers as a medicine bottle, with God pouring out a measured spoonful in the confident assurance that, even though the child might complain, he would "get better" because of it.

Marge's argument that Satan might be behind everything was discussed, and the group decided they'd better not put this on the portrait. For one thing, no passages Marge had found developed the thought. And in two of the incidents where Satan was most closely connected to trials (Job, and Paul's "thorn in the flesh"), Scripture made it clear that while Satan *intended* to make trouble, God, behind the scenes, was using the situation for His good purposes. Somehow Satan couldn't seem to slip anything over on God. So, for this particular picture, they left him out. Marge didn't mind. Her ideas had been considered seriously — and she *had* contributed the idea of the bitter medicine.

The insights from Habakkuk were harder to visualize, till Herb, the literary one, remembered a poem he'd memorized years before. "I'm not sure this is word perfect," he apologized, "but it goes something like this:

> Whenever Richard Cory went to town
> the people on the pavement gazed at him.

He was a gentleman from soul to crown,
     clean favored, and imperially slim.
And he was rich, yes, richer than a king,
     and admirably schooled in every grace.
In fine we thought that he was everything
     to make us wish that we were in his place.

So on we worked, and went without the cake
     and cursed the bread,
And Richard Cory one fine summer's night
     went home and put a bullet through his head.

"Richard Cory"
Edward Arlington
Robinson

"I think," Herb said, "the poet was saying something like Habakkuk is saying. We look on the outside, and the successful or rich man seems to have it made. But we can't tell what's going on inside. We can't tell the emptiness, the despair, that life may involve.

"I guess the Bible is saying that whenever sin is at the root of success or striving, it makes a Richard Cory of us. We've got everything — but there's no satisfaction."

So the group, in a more serious mood, drew a sketch of Richard Cory at the bottom of their portrait. And somehow any envy they had felt seemed to die with him.

To the group, this portrait seemed to symbolize the main factual elements of the biblical revelation; to summarize God's view of the "success of the wicked." And to reveal the reality of how things are working and do work in our world.

Toward Response

When we begin to understand a life situation from God's perspective, we discover that such understanding always carries action implications. Seeing reality always places unique demands on us to respond; to bring our thoughts and feelings and lives into harmony with God. [1]

Responding to God as guided by Scripture is always a freeing experience. Jesus presents this thought when speak-

[1] Chapters 6 through 9 are important background for this chapter. They not only develop the idea of Scripture as a portrait of reality, they also help explain *how* it's possible for us to actually begin to bring our thoughts, feelings, and lives into harmony with God.

ing to those who had believed in Him. "If you continue in my word, you are truly my disciples, and you will know the truth, and the truth shall make you free" (John 8:31, 32). Coming to know the truth through experience, by "continuing in His Word" (or, as the *Living New Testament* puts it, "if you live as I tell you to"), leads us toward freedom. Freedom to respond to life in ways that we know will help us and others — not hurt. Freedom to walk forward, knowing that illusion hasn't blinded us to hidden disaster. We are freed by an inner confidence that we are acting in harmony with God's will, led within by the gentle voice of the Holy Spirit, and without by the solid objective portrait of reality in the Word. When Spirit and Word agree, we ·are free to act, knowing that God is with us.

It was to action implications that the conversation at Jerry's house now turned. Because each had learned that the others loved and accepted him as he was, and were eager to support him, each felt free to share ways God had spoken to his heart through the Word.

Herb began, and with growing insight told what he was discovering about himself. He'd come to see his reaction to being passed over for the promotion as a mixture of anger and envy. His physical reaction, he felt, was partly due to his struggle to hold in the anger he was unwilling to admit — even to himself. Now, seeing his reaction for what it was, and recognizing its roots in his repressed fury, Herb was ready to share his problem with others and bring it honestly to God. "It's funny," he said. "But I can see now that instead of anger, I ought to be feeling compassion for him. If life really works as the Bible says, he's the one who's in trouble, not me!"

Herb's problem wasn't solved that night. But over the next weeks, as the others prayed for him and as he shared what was happening at the plant, his perception of the situation, his attitude toward his rival and his boss, and even his feelings about them, did change. God was working through His Word and through His Body to transform.

While the study had helped Jerry, too, he was still uncertain about his problem with the Christian who had defrauded him. Toward the end of the discussion that evening, when they sketched their portrait of reality, Jerry had objected.

"But isn't my case different? I mean, we're talking about the wicked. I guess that means the unsaved, doesn't it? Does the same thing work out for a Christian?"

Jerry's doubts launched the group on another study of Scripture. How *does* God deal with the believer who has stepped out of line? What can the Christian do to help a brother? If we're in the same Body, don't we have a special responsibility to help him back to a closer walk with God?

They discovered some challenging truths in Scripture that brought all of them up short. And it took a lot of hard praying before Jerry could gather the courage to act on what he discovered in the Word. But he did act.

Each began to.

And in the process, each began to discover what life is all about.

For life with God is to be an adventure for all of us. An adventure that challenges us, that stretches us out beyond our capacities, that demands a level of dedication lost to most of Christ's Church today. An adventure that rewards the believer who learns to live "by the Word" and "with the Body" in peace and joy and longsuffering and goodness and gentleness and — with transformation.

FOLLOW THROUGH

1. *Individual before meeting,* study the passages and insights others gained in their personal Bible study, as recorded on page 124 (4). From them, try drawing your own "reality portrait" in the space provided on next page.

2. *Individual before meeting,* after drawing your reality portrait, complete the *action implications* sections of this chapter's worksheet.

3. *When you meet,* share your ideas and construct together a group "portrait of reality" as related to your concern. Then share the insights you have into action implications appropriate to your understanding of reality (worksheet on page 134).

4. See FOLLOW THROUGH #1 (p. 144) and agree on a book to study in preparation for your next meeting.

WORKSHEET Chapter 12

1. In the following space, make a sketch of the biblical portrait of reality as related to your group's concern.

PORTRAYING REALITY

2. Think of several specific personal incidents or experiences in your area of concern (both those you may have shared with the group and some you may not have mentioned, or thought of later). Jot down the incidents, and they complete the *action implication* chart below.

Incident or experience	How I responded (thought, felt, acted)	Response appropriate to reality (thoughts, feelings, actions)

II. Building Understanding

The Bible, the Book of Life. It's good to know how to search out its perspective when life forces questions and concerns upon us.

But our needs aren't always our concerns. Often we're not even aware when our attitudes, our feelings, or our actions reflect a misunderstanding of reality. As the Bible puts it, "there is a way that seems right to a man, but the end thereof are the ways of death." The Christian's lifelong task is to pattern his life on ways that seem right to God — not to man.

We saw in the first chapters that Tom, in seeking guidance in Scripture, worked from a *basic knowledge of the Word.* The problem we now must face is this: how can a person build a basic knowledge of the Word of God? How can we start with Scripture, and, working systematically, build understanding of God's viewpoint? How can we discover more and more of His understanding of reality, submitting ourselves to His authority through the Word?

Such Bible study, like the search for light on a pressing concern, is best done with others. Together. Seeing a passage through others' eyes; digging together to interpret a difficult passage; exploring the impact of discovered truth on personal experience — all these are enriched by sharing with others in Christ's Body who together are committed to living — not merely learning about — God's Word.

Principles

Section 1.

Seek to live Scripture, not just learn about it.
Section 2.
LIFE AT ISSUE: to go from life's concerns to find God's
guidance in Scripture . . .
10. Define a shared *concern.*
11. Search for *several* relevant Scripture *passages.*
12. Let the *biblical perspective* guide your *response.*
BUILDING UNDERSTANDING: to start from Scripture to seek
God's perspective on life . . .
13. Gain an overview of *developed thought.*

13
An Initial Approach

The existence of a concern that drives us to
Scripture, discussed in the last three chapters, does more than motivate study.
It provides a focus for our study. The
concern sets a goal, gives a framework
to the search. In short, it determines
how we go about our study.

What provides this focus when we come
to Scripture without any particular concern? What gives us the framework,
the goal, that determines how we can best
study Scripture to build understanding?

We saw it earlier in the book. The idea that the Bible is
written in units of *developed* thought. Not in snatches.

If the Bible were written in snatches, probably an appropriate method of study would be to open it at random
and read until something struck us. Then we could think
about it, apply it, and later open to another page and do
the same.

But the Bible *isn't* written in snatches, with disorganized
thoughts scattered at random through its pages. Most of the
Bible is written in longer or shorter units of thought that
have their own coherent logic. And it's this *development of
thought,* this *logic of God's revelation,* that determines our
approach to Scripture when trying to build understanding
of the Word of God.

In saying that the Bible is written in developed units of
thought, I'm not suggesting that Scripture is all organized
the same way. Or that each unit of thought is the same
number of chapters long, or built on the same logic. As a
matter of fact, biblical thought is developed in a variety
of ways.

Earlier we looked at the book of Job, and saw a whole
book organized around a single theme. The Old Testament
book of Jeremiah is organized differently. It records a number of Jeremiah's sermons, with historical incidents and seg-

ments inserted. To understand Jeremiah, to follow its developed thought, we have to study each sermon as a separate unit, yet one which contributes to the impact of the whole and is understood by placing it in its historical setting.

Other books are developed in still different ways. The first books of the Old Testament, and Acts in the New, are built on the logic of historical sequence. They're organized to follow events through time, and the sequence of events is important in understanding them. Many of the New Testament books are letters. But even letters differ. Romans is a strictly logical letter, with each thought flowing rigorously from the preceding as the apostle Paul presents a carefully reasoned exposition of the doctrine of salvation. First Corinthians, which follows Romans in our Bibles, is also a letter, but a "problem solving" letter. Here Paul takes up a series of questions the Church at Corinth has relayed to him. So instead of a unified, logical doctrinal dissertation we have a disjointed response to seven problems, each one (and thus each shift of topic) marked in the text by the phrase "now concerning."

The variety of the Bible, which is one source of its richness as literature, should be recognized by the believer who studies it. While the variety may seem confusing at first, [1] it's helpful to remember that each book, each segment, still does exhibit a basic characteristic: *it presents developed thought.* Because this is the way the Bible is written, in units of thought, it's this way that we must approach it if we are to understand its message. That is, as our fifth study principle suggests, we need to get an overview of, and then to examine closely, Scripture's development of thoughts and ideas.

Here's how we can go about it:

Broadly Outlining a Bible Portion

Since we're planning to deal with developed thought, we want to get an overview of any book we plan to study.

There are several ways to do this. One is to look for a word or phrase that occurs over and over in the book, and

[1] Guidelines for putting each book of the Bible in its historical setting and pointers to its particular logic of development are included in chapter 16 of this book.

1 Simon Peter, a servant and apostle of Jesus Christ,
To those who have obtained a faith of equal standing with ours in the righteousness of our God and Savior Jesus Christ:[a]
2 May grace and peace be multiplied to you in the knowledge of God and of Jesus our Lord.

3 His divine power has granted to us all things that pertain to life and godliness, through the knowledge of him who called us to[b] his own glory and excellence, 4 by which he has granted to us his precious and very great promises, that through these you may escape from the corruption that is in the world because of passion, and become partakers of the divine nature. 5 For this very reason make every effort to supplement your faith with virtue, and virtue with knowledge, 6 and knowledge with self-control, and self-control with steadfastness, and steadfastness with godliness, 7 and godliness with brotherly affection, and brotherly affection with love. 8 For if these things are yours and abound, they keep you from being ineffective or unfruitful in the knowledge of our Lord Jesus Christ. 9 For whoever lacks these things is blind and shortsighted and has forgotten that he was cleansed from his old sins. 10 Therefore, brethren, be the more zealous to confirm your call and election, for if you do this you will never fall; 11 so there will be richly provided for you an entrance into the eternal kingdom of our Lord and Savior Jesus Christ.

12 Therefore I intend always to remind you of these things, though you know them and are established in the truth that you have. 13 I think it right, as long as I am in this body,[c] to arouse you by way of reminder,

(margin annotations:) "effort" & "escape" means pressures? trials?

God's action

us!

sort of how we apply what God's done?

Figure 8

Column of Second Peter 1, showing preliminary study: underlining and annotation. Wide margin study Bibles can be obtained from the American Bible Society.

see if this gives insight into the theme of the book. Repetition isn't always a certain clue. For instance, the book of First Peter (which we'll use in these chapters as an example of the *building understanding* approach) frequently brings in the thought of suffering, and uses seven different words for suffering in five brief chapters. But Peter's developed thought doesn't seem to hinge around suffering. James, on the other hand, constantly uses the word "faith," and it becomes clear as we read the book that his developed thought *is* organized around this theme.

Recurrent words and *recurrent ideas,* then, are something to look for as we read through a book for clues to its theme.

The best way to get an impression of the theme of a book or passage is to read it through several times, underlining or marking sections that seem significant (see Figure 8). After several readings, it's usually possible to sketch the broad outlines of the book.

Perhaps the best way to record one's impression of the general development of a book or passage is with an outline. The outline then forms a skeleton for further study of the book, a framework within which to locate each paragraph and each thought.

What might the preliminary outline of a book look like? Here's an example: a simple outline of First Peter growing out of the kind of observations illustrated in Figure 8.

FIRST PETER

Intro	1:1-2	
Part One	HEAVENLY HOLDINGS	1:1 - 2:10
	I. Assured by God	1:3-4
	II. Applied by men	1:5 - 2:10
Part Two	PRESENT PILGRIMAGE	2:11 - 4:19
	I. Pathway outlined	2:11 - 3:7
	II. Implications of pathway	3:8 - 4:11
Part Three	ETERNAL EXPECTATIONS	5:1-11
Personal greetings	5:12-14	

Making a Detailed Outline

There are several values in outlining. Working out an outline in our first approach to a book or passage helps us be sure that we're reading and interpreting in the framework of the developed thought of the Word itself. Often seeing a verse *in the context of its passage* is the key to interpreting it.

For instance, in dialog with a rich young man, Jesus answered a question: "What shall I do to inherit eternal life?" Jesus response? "One thing you lack. Sell all that you have and distribute to the poor, and you will have treasure in heaven; come, and follow me" (Mark 10:17f).

Are we to sell all that we have in obedience to this command? Is this Jesus' own prescription for eternal life? Taken out of context, we might so understand these words. Church history testifies to the fact that men *have* drawn just these conclusions, both in Catholic monasticism and in Protestant sects. But such conclusions are drawn without attention to context.

When we look at the command in context, we see it as a singular statement made for a specific purpose. The young man had asked what he could *do* to inherit eternal life. Jesus' reference to the commandments of God had brought the response, "All this I have done from my youth." Here was a person who, as far is he knew, was qualified. He had kept the commandments; he had earned eternal life.

Jesus' next statement cut through the curtain of self-righteousness that blocked the young man's view of reality. In Law, the first and great commandment is, "Thou shalt love the Lord thy God with all thine heart. . . ." And the commandments also stated, "Thou shalt have no gods before me." Jesus' challenge confronted the youth with a direct command from the God he felt he loved fully: "sell all you have." Forced to choose between his God and his wealth, he made a jolting discovery. "He became very sad," the text tells us, "for he was very rich." He turned away. Jesus' demand had exposed reality: his heart, like that of every one of us, was warped with sin. There was nothing he could *do* to inherit life; sin's grip on heart and will would not permit him to respond to God.

In the context of the passage's developed thought, Christ's command can be understood. It is not a general prescription for every man; it was a unique ministry of conviction which He performed for one wealthy man and, through him, for all whose lives are centered on possessions rather than on the Lord.

Outlining the book or passage defines the context. It helps protect us from interpreting God's Word out of context, and without awareness of His purpose in speaking it.

In studying the Bible to build understanding, we need always to keep the developed thought in clear focus.

Other values of outlining appear as we go into more detail. For detailed outlines not only trace the theme; they give us specific understanding of how the theme is developed. For instance, notice how much more information the developed outline of First Peter gives us than the preliminary outline did. And notice how it helps us follow the progression of thought in each major section (Figure 9).

We make a detailed outline by following the same procedure as for working out a preliminary one. Only we work within sections, and try to show the progression of thought and argument. Reading and rereading a section, marking what seems significant to us in the text or margin, is the best way to work toward the detailed outline.

It's helpful to remember that, while the Word of God is inspired, our outlines are not. People differ as to how they see and outline the development of thought in a book or passage. This is another reason why it's helpful to study the Bible with others. Then we profit from what they see; we check our insights and observations against theirs, and all of ours against the objective Word.

In studying the Bible this way with others there are several things to remember.

(1) As in researching a shared concern, we need to study individually before we meet. Preparation, personal exposure to God's Word and to His voice, is part of our responsibility to others in the Body. In small group and family Bible study, there's not a single teacher whose interpretation each one is bound to accept, and who alone is responsible to prepare. In shared study, the Holy Spirit is our Teacher, and the Word of God is the objective authority to which each of us must submit his understanding.

(2) Sharing of discovery in systematic Bible study should involve sharing the *process of discovery* as well as the *product*. We don't come to the group simply to present and

FIRST PETER

Intro   1:1-2

Part One:

HEAVENLY HOLDINGS 1:1 - 2:10 (Ours in Christ)
I. Assured by God 1:3-4
II. Applied by men 1:5 - 2:10
    A. to trials . . . consolation   1:6-13
    B. to temptation . . . consecration 1:13 - 2:3
    C. to daily living . . . concentration 2:4-10

Part Two:

PRESENT PILGRIMAGE 2:11 - 4:19 (Ours for Christ)
    I. Pathway outlined 2:11 - 3:7
       A. submission to God (personal)   2:11-12
       B. submission to rulers (civil)   2:13-17
       C. submission to masters (social)   2:18-25
       D. submission to mates (familial)   3:1-7
   II. Implications of pathway 3:8 - 4:11
       A. the common course (peace)   3:8-13
       B. the uncommon course
                    (suffering)   3:14-22
         1 — its result
         2 — our response
         3 — the principle
         4 — our example
         5 — God's purpose
       C. the compelling challenge   4:1-11
       D. a parenthetical warning   4:12-19

Part Three:

ETERNAL EXPECTATIONS 5:1-11
    I. Service rewarded 5:1-4
   II. The submissive exalted 5:5-7
  III. The steadfast glorified 5:8-11
Personal greetings   5:12-14

Figure 9
Developed Outline of First Peter

argue for our particular outline. We want to share the insights we've gained, the thoughts and observations which led us to our present outlines. And when something in God's Word has challenged us, or convicted us, or thrilled us as we studied, we want to share this too.

(3) As noted above, our outlines are *not* inspired. They are our personal and preliminary understanding of the development of thought in a book or passage. As we go deeper into the Scripture portion, our view may change. We may see things that escaped us in our initial reading and re-reading.

It's good to remember this. Too often when believers study the Bible with others to seek information (in contrast to sharing a concern), the discussion deteriorates to argument. One person attempts to convince others to see things his way, and rejects their insights and ideas. *This attitude is entirely out of place when believers study Scripture together.* We gather not to convince, but to share. To be open to insights God may give others, and to openly share our own understandings. And to rely on God to guide us to an accurate grasp of His truth.

We can afford to adopt this attitude. For we have a sure Word of God, an authoritative Word, and His Spirit to guide us to understanding. As we search out His counsels, seek to trace His thoughts on the pages of Scripture, and willingly submit ourselves to obey His voice, He will guide us to a unique and fresh perspective on life — His Own.

FOLLOW THROUGH

1. *Individual before meeting:* do preliminary study to develop a tentative outline of a Bible book. Headstart help is provided on worksheets for the book of James. Or your group may decide to study another book after looking over Chapter 6.
2. *When you meet,* discuss what you discovered in your study (worksheet #2, #4).
   Optional: work out a consensus outline of the book you are studying for all group members to use as you go on.

1. Locate a word or words repeated a number of times. (If you are studying James, the key word is "faith.") *Underline* each occurence in your Bible, and record below observations on how the word is used in this book.

_____

_____

_____

_____

_____

_____

2. Reread your book or passage two or three times, *underlining* and making notes in the margin (see Figure 8, p. 139).
3. Make a preliminary outline of the book, filling in as many details as you wish (Figure 9, p. 143) shows a developed outline. If you are studying James, work with the basic outline below, filling in details.

JAMES

Theme: A Living Faith

I.   The practice of a living faith (1:2 - 2:13)

II.   The principles of a living faith (2:14-26)

III.   The problems of a living faith (3:1 - 4:17)

IV.   The prospects/promises of a living faith (5:1-19)

4. Jot down any discoveries that seem particularly relevant to your own life as you read in James.

AN INITIAL APPROACH

Principles

Section 1.

    Seek to live Scripture, not just learn about it.
Section 2.

        LIFE AT ISSUE: to go from life's concerns to find God's
                guidance in Scripture . . .
10. Define a shared *concern.*
11. Search for *several* relevant Scripture *passages.*
12. Let the *biblical perspective* guide your *response.*
      BUILDING UNDERSTANDING: to start from Scripture to seek
                God's perspective on life . . .
13. Gain an overview of *developed thought.*
14. *Follow thought* closely by *paraphrasing.*

14
Crystallizing Understanding

The ultimate goal of our study of God's Word is to let His portrait of reality so shape our perceptions, our feelings, our attitudes, that our lives become clear reflections of His will. For this to happen we need to understand Scripture's portrayal; we need a grasp of what God is saying to us.

Sketching the development of a passage or book of Scripture by making an outline is a first step toward understanding God's revelation. The next step? Go into an outlined portion to crystallize our understanding of what we have read.

Probably the best way to do this in through *paraphrasing*. That is, by trying to put *the thought of the passage* in *your own words*. Both italicized phrases are important. The first emphasizes our goal: to grasp the thought of the biblical passage, its meaning. The second emphasizes our method: by finding fresh words or phrases not used in the text which convey its meaning.

Paraphrasing, then, involves us in an intensive search for meaning, and in a creative search for a fresh way to express it. When we search carefully, we find Scripture opening up to us in an astoundingly vital way.

How do we start to paraphrase? Let's see by working on a sample passage in First Peter (3:14-22).

We begin by *locating* the passage, using our developed outline of the book. Looking at the outline (page 143) shows us that this passage is part of a larger unit of developed thought. And we see that the larger unit is talking about what happens when a believer follows God's pathway in relation to various authorities: submission. The particular part of the outline that helps us locate our passage is Part II.

147

The discussion just before 3:14-22 (II. A. on the outline) teaches that the usual outcome when a believer lives in harmony with divine, governmental, and interpersonal authority (by willingly submitting to them) is peace and blessing. "Who is there to harm you if you are zealous for what is right," the argument concludes. And through it all it points us to a sovereign God who has His eyes constantly on the righteous, and who is ever attentive to their prayers.

With the passage *located* in the context of the book's development, we can begin to paraphrase. Figure 10 shows the RSV text on the left (marked earlier in preliminary study done when developing the outline), and the paraphrase on the right. Read them both, and then we'll go on to see how the paraphrase was arrived at.

RSV text	Paraphrase

RSV text

14 But even if you do suffer for righteousness' sake, you will be blessed. Have no fear of them, nor be troubled, 15 but in your hearts reverence Christ as Lord. Always be prepared to make a defense to any one who calls you to account for the hope that is in you, yet do it with gentleness and reverence; 16 and keep your conscience clear, so that, when you are abused, those who revile your good behavior in Christ may be put to shame. 17 For it is better to suffer for doing right, if that should be God's will, than for doing wrong. 18 For Christ also died[h] for sins once for all, the righteous for the unrighteous, that he might bring us to God, being put to death in the flesh but made alive in the spirit; 19 in which he went and preached to the spirits in prison, 20 who formerly did not obey, when God's patience waited in the days of Noah, during the building of the ark,

Paraphrase

Sometimes you may get in trouble for doing the right thing—but even that will work out for your good. If it happens, (1) don't be afraid of them, (2) don't get upset, (3) remember that Christ is Lord —He's still in charge! (4) Be ready to calmly and respectfully explain to anyone who questions you about your optimistic outlook while suffering and (5) keep your conscience clean. Then when you are insulted and slandered for being a Christian, your open and honest way of life will embarrass them.

in which a few, that is, eight persons, were saved through water. 21 Baptism, which corresponds to this, now saves you, not as a removal of dirt from the body but as an appeal to God for a clear conscience, through the resurrection of Jesus Christ, 22 who has gone into heaven and is at the right hand of God, with angels, authorities, and powers subject to him.

Remember — it's your own fault if you suffer for doing wrong; its much better to do right. If you suffer for that, you'll know it's by God's special choice.

It was just like this with Christ. Once He even died because of sins, the blameless One instead of the ones who deserved it. But for a purpose: to bring us to God, His body being put to death, His spirit bringing Him to life again. . . .

(Wow! The rest of this is *hard!*)

Figure 10
Paraphrase of I Peter 3:14-22

Arriving at a Paraphrase

A glance at the paraphrase (Figure 10) shows several phrases that highlight thoughts not brought out by the rsv text. This, of course, is one of the chief values of paraphrasing — to discover and express fresh insights into the text. To restate the passage in a way that *does* highlight your new understanding.

But it may be hard to see that some of the paraphrased thoughts really do "say the same thing" as the original text. For instance, are these two really saying the same thing?

RSV	Paraphrase
For it is better to suffer for doing right, if that should be God's will, than for doing wrong.	Remember—it's your own fault if you suffer for doing wrong. It's much better to do right. If you suffer for that, you'll know it's by God's special choice.

Actually, the paraphrase is an *interpretation* of the text. Most *translations* of the Bible (such as the King James, Revised Standard Version, American Revised Version, etc.) stay as close to the original Greek and Hebrew as possible, and rigorously choose words that parallel the original ones.

149

A *paraphrase,* unlike a translation, does not attempt to duplicate words and thoughts, but to interpret them, to rephrase them to highlight meaning. Paraphrasing then goes beyond the text, and says, "Here is what the text *means.*"

The question to ask in comparing a paraphrase to the biblical text, then, is "Does it accurately express the meaning?" So we need to ask, does "it is better to suffer for doing right, etc." *mean* "it's your own fault if you suffer for doing wrong. It's much better to do right. If you suffer from doing that, you'll know it's by God's special choice."

We can discover this by seeing how we arrived at the meaning — and how you can go about paraphrasing yourself to arrive at meaning. The basic steps are really quite simple:

(1) *Pay careful attention to context.* We've seen that the passage as a whole focuses our attention on the unusual case of a person doing the right thing and suffering for it. And so any paraphrase ought to highlight that particular focus.

(2) *Notice repeated emphases in the passage.* What's striking in this passage is the stress put on the sovereignty of God ("Christ as *Lord*" v. 15; "by God's will," v. 17; Christ's resurrection supremacy over all authorities, v. 22). Somehow the idea that God is actively, personally, and sovereignly involved in this particular kind of situation [when suffering follows doing right] shines through. It is these two emphases from the context of the verse that led to paraphrasing it "it's much better to do right, and then if you suffer it will be by God's special choice." *The paraphrase emphasizes what the passage seems to emphasize, to highlight its meaning.*

Paraphrasing More Difficult Sections

In most passages of Scripture, because we do have accurate translations of the original and because context is the key to all interpretation, these first two steps will probably lead you to an acceptable paraphrase. But what if you're uncertain? What if you have questions about meaning you can't solve by looking at the overall argument and emphases in the text? How do you dig deeper to find the meaning of more difficult passages?

Let's take another phrase from the First Peter 3 text and see how to arrive at its meaning:

RSV	Paraphrase
For Christ also died for sins once for all, the righteous for the unrighteous, that he might bring us to God, being put to death in the flesh but made alive in the spirit.	It was just like this with Christ. Once He even died because of sins, the blameless One instead of the ones who deserved it. But for a purpose: to bring us to God, His body being put to death, His spirit bringing Him to life again.

Let's work through the procedure and follow the first two steps already described — then go on to any others necessary to arrive at meaning.

(1) *Pay careful attention to context.* Why should Christ's death be introduced in a discussion of the unusual case when a person does the right thing, and suffers for it? Any familiarity with Christ's life and death at all suggests an obvious reason: Christ is the supreme example of this kind of situation! He *always* did the right thing, yet His obedience brought Him to the cross. He is the ultimate example of suffering for righteousness' sake.

There is also another important point in the text which Christ's death parallels. It was by God's special choice that He died for us and for our sins (Matt. 26:36-42; Acts 2:23).

(2) *Notice emphases in the text.* Repeated ideas are only one form of emphasis. Emphasis can also be grammatical, with pointers to meaning contained in connective and other words. Here emphasis that supports the idea of Christ's death being used as an example is clear in the phrase, "For Christ also. . . ." The "for" ties this topic to what has gone just before; the "also" shows clearly that the writer is presenting Christ as "another person who suffered unjustly too."

But trying to read this passage in the context of an example of unjust suffering still leaves us with problems. Look at it again:

RSV

For Christ also died for sins once for all, the righteous for the unrighteous, that he might

151

bring us to God, being put to
death in the flesh but made
alive in the spirit.

If Peter wants us to think of Christ as an example, why
use phrases like "once for all" and say that His death was
"the righteous for the unrighteous"? These phrases seem to
emphasize the nature and purpose of Christ's sacrifice: a
completed work ("once for all") of substitutionary atonement ("the righteous for the unrighteous"). Why talk about
the nature of the atonement when paralleling Christ's suffering for doing right with times when *we* suffer for doing
right? *Somehow it just doesn't seem to fit.*

It's when something in the text *doesn't seem to fit* our
understanding from context that we need to go on to take
other steps to discover meaning. "Not fitting" is the sign
that we need to dig deeper. But how?

(3) *Use various translations.* There are many translations available today. Comparing them helps us see if a
particular English rendering is demanded by the original
text, or if there are other ways of saying it that fit the Greek
and Hebrew equally well. By looking at *The Layman's Parallel New Testament* (Zondervan) which compares the King
James, Amplified, Living New Testament, and Revised Standard Versions side by side, it's clear that "once for all" is
not a necessary translation of the Greek. For the King James
and Living New Testament simply render the word, "once."
So we aren't reading here about the nature of the atonement
as a "once for all," (perfect) sacrifice! We're free to take
it simply as "For once Christ even. . . ."

(4) *Use a comprehensive concordance.* But we still have
to wrestle with the phrase, "the righteous for the unrighteous." Isn't *this* talking about the atonement; about Christ
dying for us sinners? I've often quoted it this way, as a salvation verse: "Christ died, the righteous in place of, or on
behalf of, the unrighteous." I saw it as a clear expression of
Christ taking our place on the cross. This was a *theological
interpretation* of the word "for."

But how can we tell if this understanding of the word
"for" is correct?

There are several large concordances which not only list

every appearance of each English word in the Bible, but also show the Greek or Hebrew word that it translates. Using this tool (I used a *Young's Analytical Concordance of the Bible*) to look up the word "for" we discover that it does translate several Greek and Hebrew words that mean "in behalf of" or "for the sake of." *But it also translates some thirty-eight others!* And the particular "for" in First Peter 3:18 that we're concerned about translates a Greek word meaning "on account of."

So now our passage becomes clear. Peter is saying that Christ (the righteous) died on account of the unrighteous: it was for *their* fault, not for any of His own, that He was crucified. Christ had always done the right thing. But in His case the normal course of events (in which the right thing leads to blessing and sin leads to judgment) was changed by a special choice of God — a choice that led ultimately to our acceptance by God through Christ's death and to His exaltation (v. 22). *The parallel is clear!* Christ is the example *in all points:* He did the right thing; He suffered, by God's special choice; the end result was blessing (cf. v. 14). And our paraphrase does bring out this meaning:

> It was just like this with Christ. Once He even died because of sins, the blameless One instead of the ones who deserved it. But for a purpose: to bring us to God, His body being put to death, His spirit bringing Him to life again.

In Summary

Not all paraphrasing is as difficult as this. In fact, I particularly chose a difficult passage to demonstrate how any problems you find can be solved. And to introduce some of the tools that make paraphrasing easier. The steps toward reaching a paraphrase, and the tools that help, are:

Steps	*Tools*
1. Pay careful attention to context.	1. Your outline of the book or passage.
2. Notice repeated emphases.	2. Underlining and notes in your Bible made while developing your outline.
3. Use various translations.	3. Different translations of the Bible.

4. Use a comprehensive con-cordance.	4. A concordance showing the Hebrew and Greek words which our English word translates.

In working through to the paraphrase of First Peter 3: 14-22 we've also run into common problems that you may face when you try to paraphrase, or missteps you may take in paraphrasing. These are:

(1) *Using synonyms without thinking of meaning.* Paraphrasing Scripture isn't simply substituting words. It's struggling with meaning, and, understanding meaning, creatively expressing it to highlight the biblical thought.

(2) *Ignoring connectives.* Again, the Bible is a book expressing *developed* thought. It's important when paraphasing to pay attention to connections. The particular connections we've seen in this chapter are connections of emphasis [marked by repetition of the idea of God's sovereignty] and grammatical connection [seen in constructions like "For Christ also. . . ."] which link ideas and give clues to their development.

(3) *Reading theologically.* This may seem a strange problem to mention. Actually, it's one of our greatest blocks to following the thought of the Bible. Reading theologically was illustrated by my early view that "the righteous for the unrighteous" is a statement about the substitutionary nature of Christ's atonement. *I read it this way because it fit my theology: not because I understood the writer's meaning.*

You'll find as you study the Bible that often you read theologically too — by "reading in" your theology. It's easy to do.

For example, when we evangelicals hear "saved" we automatically switch into thinking about eternal life, forgiveness of sins, and acceptance by God in Christ. But "saved" does not always refer to this when used in the Bible. In the Old Testament "saved" normally speaks of deliverance from difficulties and dangers of the present life — and it often means this in the New Testament. Reading theologically we often misunderstand New Testament passages like the Philippians 2 statement, "work out your own salvation with fear and trembling." Paraphrased we might put it, "take your difficulties seriously and dig in to find solutions!" *Salvation* here clearly means "deliverance" or "solution." What Paul is talking about isn't redemption; it's simply solving practical problems of church life.

So watch out for your theology. It may be perfectly correct theology, but not every biblical passage will use a word in its theological sense. In fact, a good rule of thumb for paraphrasing is this: *whenever you come across a term that is theologically familiar, check to see if the writer is using it the same way your theology does.* You'll be surprised to see how often he isn't!

(4) *Remember the larger context of Scripture.* This is something we talked more about in the first part of this book. Biblical ideas and phrases are not only interpreted (to be understood) by the way they're used in a book or passage — they're to be understood by the way they're used in the Bible. No passage should be interpreted in a way that contradicts the rest of the testimony of Scripture.

This principle was applied in interpreting the Philippians 2 statement above. Because the clear message of the Bible is that we receive eternal life as a free gift from God, extended to us in Jesus Christ, "work out your salvation" simply *could not* have been an exhortation to work for, to attempt to merit or earn, God's love and forgiveness. The larger context of Scripture made the use of the word here plain — and examination of the immediate context made it clear that "solution to problems" really is the meaning.

Putting together the steps to use in reaching a paraphrase, and being alert for the problems, you can work out acceptable and exciting paraphrases for much of Scripture.

The "Impossible" Passage

You probably noticed on Figure 10 (pp. 148, 149) that I did not complete the paraphrase of First Peter 3:14-22. I left out vss. 19-22 with the notation, "Wow. The rest of this is *hard!*"

I did it to indicate that sometimes you'll come across passages like this: passages that are so hard you simply cannot be sure of the meaning. And to indicate what you probably should do. Nothing. Simply give it up.

What I'm getting at is this. I honestly do believe that God's Word is given us to understand, and that therefore it is understandable. Even the difficulte passages. [1] *But this does not mean that everyone can understand everything the first time he works it through.* The Bible presents a worldview that is very different from that of our culture and society. A whole new way of thinking and looking at life; new sets of values; new understandings of how the world came into being and where history is going. There's plenty here to keep us digging all our lives without *ever* coming to understand everything.

And it's not necessary to understand everything. For we're studying the Bible, not just to learn about it, but to live it. What is necessary is to *respond to what we do understand.* To live by the light God does give us. So really, what you do come to understand of the Bible through paraphrasing is going to be much more important to you than what you don't understand. [2] And your understanding will grow, as you find that fewer and fewer passages are "impossible."

So we're back again to our true purpose in coming to the Word of God. To discover His perspective on life, and to let His Word and His will reshape our lives until we become living reflections of our Lord.

And paraphrasing is of exciting help here. Paraphrasing can be a crucial step toward translating the Word of God into your life.

FOLLOW THROUGH

1. *Individual before meeting:* work out a paraphrase of a short section in the book you are studying with your group. If you are working on James, do the passage suggested in the worksheet. It will let you use all the skills discussed in this chapter.

2. *When you meet,* share discoveries made during para-

[1] If you want to see a paraphrase of First Peter 3:19-22, I've included it on page 212.

[2] If something is really important to you, and you feel you *need* to know something you don't understand, you have several ways to find help. Since you're studying the Bible with others, you can bring your questions to the group, and see if others have discovered the meaning that eluded you. If others haven't, you can bring the questions to your pastor, for his guidance or for leads to additional resources (commentaries, etc.) which might have answers. But if something is simply a matter of curiosity, it's best not to spend a lot of time on it. Concentrate on applying what you do know to life.

phrasing, and see what others discovered in the passage. And share any questions or problems. If, *after discussion,* you are still uncertain about the meaning of James 2: 14-26, read and discuss the paraphrase of the passage included on page 211 of this book.

WORKSHEET Chapter 14

1. Locate the passage you are to paraphrase on your outline. (If your group is studying James, use 2:14-26). After looking over the outline and the passage, write a brief *general summary* of how it seems to fit in the book.

   _____

   _____

   _____

   _____

2. Look for repeated words or ideas, and try a brief definition of each *as it is used in the passage.* (For James 2: 14-26 focus on "faith" and "justified" — and watch out for the "reading theologically" trap with both!)
   Faith, as used here:

   _____

   _____

   Justified as used here:

   _____

   _____

   _____

3. Now try a paraphrase of the passage. Work out a draft on scrap paper, then record your own paraphrase of your passage here.

   _____

   _____

   _____

4. Finally, jot down any personal discoveries that seemed relevant to your own life for sharing with the group.

   _____

   _____

   _____

Principles

Section 1.

Seek to live Scripture, not just learn about it.

Section 2.

LIFE AT ISSUE: to go from life's concerns to find God's guidance in Scripture . . .

10. Define a shared *concern.*
11. Search for *several* relevant Scripture *passages.*
12. Let the *biblical perspective* shape your *response.*

BUILDING UNDERSTANDING: to start from Scripture to seek God's perspective on life . . .

13. Gain an overview of *developed thought.*
14. *Follow thought* closely by *paraphrasing.*
15. *Generalize* to *specific personal applications.*

15
Applying Discovered Truth

When we've followed the thought of the
Bible and discover its meaning we're
ready to take the last, often neglected,
step in Bible study. Discovering its
"meaning to me." As I've suggested
throughout this book, Scripture was given to
shape our lives. It's vital that we look now
to life, to discover the response God
is inviting through His gently molding
Word.

Jesus once told a simple parable of two men, a wise and
a foolish builder. The first built on solid rock, and the storms
beat futilely on his construction. The other built on sand,
and when the same storms struck, his foundationless structure was torn apart. Then Jesus made this simple application: "everyone who hears these words of mine and does
not do them will be like a foolish man who built his house
upon the sand; and the rain fell, and the floods came, and
the winds blew and beat against that house, and it fell:
and great was the fall of it" (Matt. 7:26, 27).

*The wise man builds his life on the words of God, by
doing them.* God's Word is given us to *live*, not just to learn
about.

How then do we go from the meaning of a passage to its
meaning for our lives; from the objective revelation to specific, personal application to experience?

Make a Generalization

Sometimes Scripture passages contain plain directions for
living: "Don't lie"; "Show hospitality"; "Stop gossiping," etc.
Such directions usually flow from preceding thought, marked
often by a "therefore" or "inasmuch as," and are clear guidelines for obedient response to God. But such specific applications aren't normally given in every biblical text. Scripture presents its portrait of reality, and the Holy Spirit serves

to illumine our understanding of how that reailty is to re-shape our lives.

Even when the Bible does not go to specific applications of truth, a passage will often conclude with a *generalization.* That is, it will sum up the impact on human experience of the reality it portrays by stating a *general principle:* a guide-line to action.

Peter does this in concluding his argument of First Peter 3:14-22, the passage paraphrased in the last chapter.

Making a generalization is the first step in moving from Scripture to life. Summing up the impact of the Bible's view of reality on human experience is essential if we're to begin living in response to God's Word.

While not every unit of developed thought in Scripture includes a generalization, a great number do. Where none is included, we need to make the generalization ourselves. A simple process will help us:

(1) *Isolate key thoughts*
If do right then suffer, will be blessed.
Christ is *Lord.*
If suffer for doing right, it's God's special will — in-tended for special good.

(2) *Summarize*
God really is in control, supervising the outcome of all choices we make. *We are free then to do God's will,* knowing if suffering should result [but usually won't] that He has a pur-pose for good in view.

(3) *Generalization*
Let's choose to live by God's will, and make our decisions solely on what's right — not under pressure from the desires that usu-ally control decision-mak-ing.

Following this simple procedure of isolating the key thoughts in a passage, unifying them in a summary, and then making a generalization to life helps us begin to re-cast Scripture as life.

List Varied Applications

I've suggested in another book [1] that "every person lives in his own particular situation, in a whole complex of relationships and personality that make his life uniquely *his.* Thus each individual has special opportunities to use a Bible truth, his own special areas of need."

The plurals here are important. We each have *opportunities* to apply Scripture. We each have *areas* of need. Each general principle we draw from Scripture has multiple application to each of our lives. And it has *concrete* application.

Too often we're satisfied when studying the Bible to stop with generalization. "We need to live by God's will. Wonderful! Let's do it!" But generalizations are not *usable.* They're not specific enough, concrete enough, personal enough, actually to result in an obedient response. To bring Bible discoveries into the realm of experience and to spell out clearly specific opportunities, each of us has to live by the Word. This is essential. *We need to define those areas of life which discovered truth affects.*

Probably the best way to do this is by making a list of varied applications; by pinpointing as many different areas of impact on life as possible. Thus to get varied applications of the general principle derived from the study of First Peter 3 [make decisions solely by God's will — by what is right], we might begin by thinking of the kind of decisions we make. For an individual, the process might be something like this:

✿　✿　✿　✿　✿　✿　✿　✿

Decisions. Hmm. What kind of decisions do I make? Well, there's big decisions — wife, job, where to send the kids to school, buying a house or car, changing jobs. And how about daily decisions? Let's see. . . . Use of time, I guess. How much TV, time with the family, reading, time

[1] *Creative Bible Teaching,* Moody Press, 1970.

161

for God? Work I bring home. Money. That's a big one. How do I spend my money? Giving? How about that new fishing outfit? Why do I want to buy that? You know, sometimes I buy things for the kids just to shut them up. Not a good reason. Bad, really. Other relationships too. My boss. Do I shade reports sometimes, to make me look better? Is that honest? Why do I do it? And time for others. Why did I cut off Madge when I knew she wanted to talk about her mother? And that invitation to teach Sunday school. To work on club committees. . . . Man, this is beginning to pinch!

✿ ✿ ✿ ✿ ✿ ✿ ✿ ✿

When we set out to generate a list of different ways a truth might apply to life we *do* get down to where the truth hurts. But we also open up our lives to the Holy Spirit, inviting Him to enter our lives and evaluate them, focusing our attention on those areas He particularly wants to be marked by a fresh responsiveness to God.

The process of developing a list of varied applications (like the other processes suggested in this chapter) are best done in company with others. For as we share our lives with them, and they share with us, fresh insights are born, and we each see new relationships of God's Word to our experience.

So then: the first step in applying discovered truth to our life is to make a generalization. The second step is to list varied applications.

Personalize

The third step is one that we've already begun. It's looking over the broad range of *possible* applications of discovered truth, and focusing on those areas where it is most relevant to us. In this process we discover the response which God invites each of us as individuals to make to Him: the particular way each life is to be rebuilt on the foundation of obedience to His words.

Many applications generated by a group will seem "out there" to us — relevant enough for others, but not particularly vital to our own experience. When we're studying the Bible privately, the process of working though to varied applications will lead us quickly to sensitive areas in our lives.

How do we move in our group from "out there" applications to our own needs for fresh response to God? It's important here that our discussion take on the character of sharing. That is, that we shift from talking about *ideas* [here's a way it might apply to someone] to begin speaking of our *experience* [I've faced this issue in . . .]. Such sharing can be stimulated by talking over questions like the following, and opening up our lives to the others: How have I responded in the past when faced with this kind of issue — and what happened? What situations or decisions do I face that this truth helps me evaluate — and how will I respond?

The result?

Sharing our lives with others. Seeking and giving support and encouragement as decisions to act on God's Word are expressed.

And really, this is the purpose for which God has called His Church together. To live in unity, as a Body, sharing a common life in Christ, and encouraging one another to live lives that will progressively become more and more a reflection of God's Own.

When a sharing group takes the Word of God as central to their life together, Word and Body together become the Spirit's tools of transformation.

In Summary

To learn God's Word for living we want to seek the company of other committed Christians, and join with them in a search to understand and respond to Scripture. After outlining a biblical unit of thought, we paraphrase a segment to discover meaning. When we've grasped the meaning of a passage of Scripture, we move on to application by the process outlined in Figure 11. *(Generalizing — Varied application — Personalizing — Deciding response)*.

While not every passage of Scripture that we study will lead directly to a specific response for each individual, the general principle we operate on in all Bible study is this: God's Word *is* for living. We seek to learn God's Word to live in obedience to it.

And somehow, the more clearly we grasp God's biblical portrayal of reality, the more our thoughts and our feelings and our viewpoints become those God has shared with us in His Word — and the more our lives change. The more

The Process of Applying Discovered Truth

1. Generalization: statement of principle	2. Varied applications: areas of life to which principle applies	3. Personalization: area most relevant to personal needs	4. Determination: how I will seek to apply this week
Let's choose to live by God's will and make decisions on what is right.	Decisions I make . . . wife job car kids school buy house time use — TV — family time — reading — time for God? — work brought home		This week I'll . . .
		time for family, God. (do I bring too much work home? priorities?)	
	money — fishing outfit? — giving — missions church — buy for kids?	why do I give in to kids "gimmees"? Cheap love? It's not really *best for them*.	start saying *no* when its best for kids.
	relationships — boss (honest reports?) — Madge — cut her off Th. SS class? time for club?	Madge was upset, and I didn't care enough to listen. God cares — I should too.	apologize to Madge, invite her to lunch and let her know I'll listen

our lives are lived in joyful responsiveness to a God whose will we have come to *know*.

FOLLOW THROUGH

1. *Individual before class,* work through a fresh portion of Scripture for sharing at the next group meeting. If your group is studying James, focus on the short segment, James 3:13-18. The worksheet will guide you through the application process.

2. *When you meet,* share discoveries made paraphrasing the passage and agree on its meaning. Together state a *generalization,* and develop a list of varied applications. Finally, share personal experience and specific situations in which you will have opportunities to act in this Word from God.

APPLYING DISCOVERED TRUTH

1. On separate sheets of paper follow the procedure outlined in the last chapter to work out a paraphrase of your new passage. If your group is studying James, do James 3:13-18.

2. To prepare for group discussion of the meaning of discovered truth to your lives,

   A. Make a tentative generalization from the passage you have just studied.

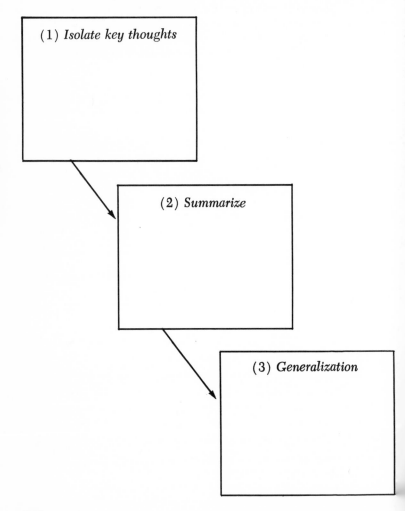

(1) *Isolate key thoughts*

(2) *Summarize*

(3) *Generalization*

CREATIVE BIBLE STUDY

B. List as many areas of application of the general principle (A3) as you can think of. (See "varied applications" on Figure 11.)

_____

_____

_____

_____

_____

_____

_____

_____

C. Personalize by jotting down experiences you've had, or situations you face, in which the truth discovered is particularly pertinent to you.

_____

_____

_____

_____

_____

_____

_____

_____

3. When you meet, share your ideas of the way the Word will apply to your life. And beforehand ask God's guidance to specific responses He may be inviting you to make to His Word.

_____

_____

_____

_____

_____

_____

_____

_____

_____

_____

_____

Principles

Section 1.

Seek to live Scripture, not just learn about it.

Section 2.

LIFE AT ISSUE: to go from life's concerns to find God's guidance in Scripture . . .

10. Define a shared *concern*.

11. Search for *several* relevant Scripture *passages*.

12. Let the *biblical perspective* shape your *response*.

BUILDING UNDERSTANDING: to start from Scripture to seek God's perspective on life . . .

13. Gain an overview of *developed thought*.

14. *Follow thought* closely by *paraphrasing*.

15. *Generalize* to *specific personal applications*.

Section 3.

RESOURCES: to develop a grasp of broader principles of Bible study . . .

16. Locate passages in their *Scriptural framework*.

Section Three:
RESOURCES

You've now completed the action part of this book. If you're engaged in a 20-week trial group study (as suggested at the beginning), 17 of your 20 meetings are over. What of the last three? You have several choices: agree on a new book to study; continue to study in James; or focus on a new concern, using the approach developed in chapters 10 - 13. If you're using this book in a thirteen-week class study, you have six weeks left: time for both a "concern" and a book study.

Perhaps these resource chapters will help you choose how to use the remaining time — and to decide if you want to continue meeting after the trial period is over. What resources does it contain?

Chapter 17, "The Framework of Revelation," helps orient you to the place of each book of Scripture in its historical setting, and highlights its special contributions. And it locates key passages and events, and major units of thought. Looking the chapter over, you'll find that some books will be particularly interesting to you — and these you may choose to study first.

Chapter 18 shares a list of ten typical concerns to which the Bible speaks, and gives starter suggestions for your study: major passages, key words for concordance study, relevant Biblical characters, etc. The list is merely suggestion: your group will probably want to locate and study its own special concerns and needs. But the list may stimulate your thinking — and suggest avenues for individual Bible study.

Chapter 19 surveys some of the books that are helpful tools for Bible study. It comments on their values — and limitations. For tools are only tools: it is the Word itself that we are to study.

Only the Word has, and gives us, life.

16
Discovering a Living Word, Together

At this point we've developed principles
that when grasped and applied to reading
God's Word can help us discover it as
a living, vital, and transforming Word.
   One more thought remains. What is the
best context for Bible study? Where
can we expect maximum growth to take
place? For a variety of reasons, the answer
to this question is — when you study
the Bible **with others.**

When Lee joined the three of us she seemed to be an intensely shy, almost withdrawn person. We met each noon
at the base where I was stationed — Conrad, a civilian employee, Larabee, a career army sergeant, and myself, a young
sailor — to study the Bible. For two months, as we read
and talked about the book of Acts, Lee sat back in our tight
circle and didn't utter a word.

Then, slowly, Lee began to participate. She asked questions; she made comments; she began to share herself. As
her story came out, I could understand her shyness.

Lee was a divorcee with a teenaged daughter. She had
become a Christian some ten years before I met her. In
the first flush of her new faith she'd left her church, and
tried futilely to witness to her relatives. They violently rejected what she had to say. To them she seemed apostate,
one who kept on attacking them and the church. And as
their resistance stiffened, her enthusiasm began to drain.
Why weren't they able to see the Gospel as she did? Why
did they insist on staying in the awful pattern of self-effort
and ritual that had blinded her to Christ all her life?

Lee joined another church, one that seemed to know and
teach the Good News she'd heard in Christ. But she was
a divorcee. They welcomed her, but she didn't really fit.
At first the sermons were so exciting she didn't mind; there
was so much she hadn't known. But there was no warm

human fellowship — no one close to share her experiences and problems. After a few years, when the new truths became familiar, even the pastor's teaching of the Word failed to inspire.

In the years that followed, cut off from sharing with others, always aware of the barriers that kept her on the surface of life with her closest relatives, Lee settled down into a life marked by resignation and despair. She held to Christ, but the abundant life she'd dreamed of was drowned in the bitterness of reality.

And then Lee joined us, three simple believers who sat down daily to look into God's Word.

And her life began to change.

I can't explain what happened, or why. But as we read and shared together, new life seemed to flood into her. Her face brightened, her voice became strong and confident. Within a year Lee was known all over the sixth floor of the vast building where she worked as an enthusiastic and engaging person, who seemed excited about Jesus Christ and spoke freely about Him.

Together

Looking into Scripture, the conviction grows that what we four discovered, God has in mind for all of us. We're all invited to come to a Living Word, with others.

Life in Scripture, as in our experience, is always life lived with others. This isn't just because we daily brush up against them, or even because it's to others that we're privileged to express God's love. The Bible makes it plain that we need each other in our quest for life in Christ. "Just as you have many members in one physical body and those members differ in their functions, so we, though many in number, compose one body in Christ and are all members of one another" (Rom. 12:3f). We share a common life in Christ, and we have a ministry of life to one another. "The body should work together as a whole," the Bible says, "with all the members in a sympathetic relationship with one another" (1 Cor. 12:12f).

And always in the context of this idea of a common life, the Scriptures speak of "spiritual gifts" — special abilities which each of us has from God to encourage and help others.

The whole idea of "gifts" can be summed up another way: God has chosen to work in special ways through each of us, to help other believers grow in Christlikeness.

Scripture gives representative lists of these gifts in several places, notably Romans 12, First Corinthians 12, and Ephesians 4. Here and throughout the New Testament one thing is made plain: if we're to function this way, ministering to others, we can be used only when we come together in love and honesty. It's when we accept others as they are, and share ourselves as we are, that Christ's life flows through us to others.

We can be honest with other Christians, because we're not expected to be perfect. It's because we're weak and imperfect that we need the support of others! "We who have strong faith," Scripture says, "ought to shoulder the burden of the doubts and qualms of others — and not to just go our own sweet way" (Rom. 15:1f). And so we're called to become involved with others, to love them, to know them and let them know us, that we might "encourage one another to love and do good deeds" (Heb. 10:19f).

There are a number of reasons why we need to move toward honest sharing and openness with others. Perhaps the most compelling are these:

We have different gifts. Earlier I mentioned the kind of man I am; comfortable with ideas, frightened of a life that demands total involvement, emotional investment. And that my wife is different — freer to feel, and sometimes suffering just because her feelings are so strong. She has a different gift, and has ministered to me. Apart from her, and what I've gained in living with her, I could never have written this book. Apart from all God has taught me through her, the way He has forced open clogged channels of my personality, I could never be what I am today — and am becoming.

In the same way, *each one of us has a unique contribution to make to the lives of other Christians.* God, using what we are and the gift He's given, through us helps others understand themselves and taste His grace. None of us can fully become without this ministry of others. It's in "the unity of common faith and common knowledge of the Son of God" that we "arrive at real maturity — that measure of development which is meant by 'the fullness of Christ.'" All this takes place and our transformation flows through that which each of us supplies, when we live together in that warm and loving relationship which marks our common life in Him (Eph. 4:7f).

That Living Word which calls us to discover Christ in it also calls us to one another.

We need models. The life to which we're called, and that the Living Word describes, is strange to us. We haven't experienced it apart from Christ. We're used to living, and to understanding life, in far different ways than Scripture reveals. And it's doubly hard to understand a life we've never seen. We need more than words put down on paper — we need models. As the Bible says, we need to see lives that "show by contrast how dreary and futile" other ways really are.

While He was on earth Christ was a model. Men saw His life, and those who were aware of the emptiness in their own lives were drawn to Him. Only those who feared the exposure of their sin drew back. Today, too, we all desperately need to see the Gospel take form in flesh and blood.

Scripture recognizes this. We read of the young leader who is told to "be an example" in speech and behavior, in love and faith and in sincerity. He is to keep an eye on two things — life and teaching (1 Tim. 4:12f). And the old apostle Paul could write to churches he had founded and say, "model your conduct on what you have heard from me, what I have told you and shown you . . ." (Phil. 4:5f).

Not that we're expected to be perfect. Or to pretend courage we don't have, or tell of victories we haven't won. Walking in God's Light is walking honestly, and what we model is to be the Gospel. Strangely enough, it's often as we reveal our failures that we best express life in Christ. This is what Paul shows in Second Corinthians. In our weakness we know all sorts of trials. We experience our sin and bondage, and, if we live the Gospel, we turn then to Christ and come to experience His comfort. *And this whole thing, both failure and God's faithfulness, we share.*

> He gives us comfort in our trials so that we in turn may be able to give the same sort of strong sympathy to others in theirs. . . . This means that if we experience trouble we

can pass on to you comfort and spiritual help; for if we ourselves have been comforted we know how to encourage you to endure patiently the same sort of troubles that we have ourselves endured (2 Cor. 1:3f).

We reveal our weaknesses to others — that we may reveal God's strength. We share what we really are, that others may learn about themselves, and find that forgiveness strips away the shame of failure, and makes us free to trust in God.

All this we can gain from, and give to others. All this we share as we come with them to a Living Word.

Renewal

What happened in Lee's life is possible for each of us. God speaks to all in power through His Living Word. Through it His vital force moves in us, reshaping out attitudes, creating fresh emotions, clarifying belief, renewing our behavior. Transforming all we are.

And God speaks to us in others. Others who come with us to the Living Word, who strip away their masks and in the loving bond of common life in Christ, support us as we learn to trust.

ADVENTURE

Openness and honesty in personal relationships are strange to us. Even in our churches most of us have learned to hide ourselves to be accepted. So we've lived behind our masks — and come to know the emptiness of this way of life.

In our families, too, many of us have failed to find the renewing touch of love. Unable to accept and be ourselves, we've pretended with those who know us best. And discovered the bitterness and rebellion this way brings.

We need to experience openness and honesty before we can understand them — and be open and honest ourselves. It's the living taste of Truth that sets us free.

This is why each section of this book concludes with an *Adventure*. To help you explore with others the realities of which it speaks, to know by experience the Grace God pours out on us as we find, with others, a Living Word.

It may be you have read this book without others. Perhaps you have skipped over the adventures, and looked only

175

at the ideas. I hope it's helped you if you have — but still I'm sure we only realize the fullness of any truth by experiencing it. And the truth of which I've written briefly in this chapter demands experiencing.

How? Perhaps with your family. Work through the adventures together, reading the appropriate section before each meeting to talk. Perhaps three sessions a week would be about right for most families.

Another way is to meet with a group of Christian friends, who want that "fresh newness" of life the Bible offers. Eight or ten make a good sized group — just enough so you can get to know one another personally. For such a group one session a week ought to be about right. One thing though. Try to reserve at least two hours for each experience together. The traditional "one hour meeting" of the church is fine — if you don't want to know others significantly! It takes time to really get to know people.

When you meet don't bother with a "leader." Simply try out the suggestions given in each *Adventure*, and talk over each Exploration as long as you feel the need. Don't rush. In studying the Word with others you want to get to know *them* well as persons, and share their lives, as well as to look at life through Scripture. Actually you won't really reach one goal without the other. So don't hurry.

Perhaps you've done all this already. If so, go on now together to this *Adventure*.

EXPLORATION 1

> You've been together for some time now. Why not start by telling any ways that you've been helped by individuals or the group?

EXPLORATION 2

> Often in an experience like this we get insight into the gifts (those special abilities God gives each of us) of other members of the group. List beside the name of each individual in your group any gift(s) you think you've seen in them.

> Now work around the circle and let each member hear just what gifts the rest of you see in him.

EXPLORATION 3

Study Colossians 3 together. This describes the common life we are to live in Christ. Share any ways you've experienced qualities described there in your group's own fellowship.

EXPLORATION 4

What next? This series of studies is over. Now what — disband, continue? Share your feelings about this question now.

Principles

Section 1.

Seek to live Scripture, not just learn about it.

Section 2.

LIFE AT ISSUE: to go from life's concerns to find God's guidance in Scripture . . .

10. Define a shared *concern.*
11. Search for *several* relevant Scripture *passages.*
12. Let the *biblical perspective* shape your *response.*

BUILDING UNDERSTANDING: to start from Scripture to seek God's perspective on life . . .

13. Gain an overview of *developed thought.*
14. *Follow thought* closely by *paraphrasing.*
15. *Generalize* to *specific personal applications.*

Section 3.

RESOURCES: to develop a grasp of broader principles of Bible study . . .

16. Locate passages in their *Scriptural framework.*
17. Scripture is one Book; a unit woven from many.

17

The Framework of Revelation

Just as individual books of the Bible have
a pattern of developed thought, so does
the Bible as a whole. For Scripture is
one Book; a unity woven from many.
In studying any book of the Bible it's important to see how it fits into the developed
thought of the whole. To see this, it's
necessary to grasp the framework of
God's revelation.

The Scriptural revelation was shared with us by God over
a period of about two millennia. Two thousand years sep-
arates the events of Abraham's life, later recorded by Moses,
and the penning of the last book of the New Testament,
Revelation. Through the centuries God shared His understanding of reality, His purpose in history and prophecy,
His ways of working in our world — progressively. Each
word, given in a specific historical situation and speaking
to a need of His people at that time, builds on the preceding and adds to our grasp of the whole.

It's important to locate each book historically; in the context of the time and purpose for which it was given. For
that reason, the charts that follow locate books and events
in historical sequence (which is *not* the sequence of their
occurrence in our Bibles). The charts and brief comments
on each book will help you visualize the broad framework
of revelation, and provide helpful clues for studying each
book of the Bible.

THE OLD TESTAMENT

Timeline Key events	Descriptions
I. PRIMEVAL PERIOD creation — c. 2000	
GENESIS 1 - 11 creation (Ge. 1-2)	*Genesis 1 - 11* records the history of God's deal-ing with the human race. All mankind is in

Timeline	Key events	Descriptions
	fall/sin (Ge. 3-4) flood (Ge. 6-8)	view in these chapters, which have been called the "Bible in brief" because they are in the pattern of God's overall plan (creation, sin, redemption, judgment, re-creation).
JOB		*Job* gives insight into the knowledge of God which men retained through tradition, as a heritage of their common parentage. The theme of the book and its development are discussed in Chapter 10 of this book.
II. PATRIARCHAL PERIOD c. 2000 - 1900		
GENESIS 12 - 50	Covenant Promise (Ge. 12, 15, 17).	*Genesis 12 - 50* shifts focus from the race to God's dealing with one man (Abraham) and His plan through his offspring (the Jews) to bring salvation to all. God's purposes in the Jews, and His promises to them, are stated in the Abrahamic Covenant. It is this Covenant, expressing clearly God's purposes for this people, which is the unifying theme of the entire Old Testament. *The Old Testament must be understood in light of the Covenant promises.* Genesis is organized around the life of three men: Abraham (12-23), his son Isaac (13-27) and grandson Jacob, also called Israel (28-50). It records the entry of the Covenant people into Egypt.
III. EXODUS PERIOD c. 1450 - 1400		
EXODUS LEVITICUS NUMBERS DEUTERONOMY	Plagues (Ex. 1-12) Passover (Ex. 12, 13) Law (Ex. 19-23) Wilderness wandering (Nu. 11-20)	This period marks the deliverance of God's Covenant people from slavery in Egypt by acts of power and judgment. When the Israelites, brought out after 400 years in Egypt, failed to respond to God in love, Law was introduced. The Mosaic Covenant, a *conditional, temporary* covenant, determined each generation's current experience of the blessings promised in the Abrahamic Covenant. (The relationship between Abrahamic and Mosaic Covenants is shown on the next page.) The units of developed thought in these four books are:

THE EXODUS

I. *From Egypt to Sinai*   Ex. 1-18
    (1) The plagues
    (2) Crossing the sea
    (3) Traveling to Sinai

Timeline	Key events	Descriptions
		II. *Camped at Sinai* Ex. 19 - Num. 10
		(4) Law given (Ex. 19-23)
		(5) Tabernacle worship established (Ex. 24-40)
		(6) Instruction for holy living (Lev. 1:26)
		(7) Camp organized (Num. 1-10)
		III. *Wilderness wanderings* Num. 10-21
		(8) To Kadesh (Num. 10-15)
		(9) Years in wilderness (Num. 16-21)
		IV. *Camped before the promised land* Num. 22 - Deut. 34
		(10) Instructions for entering (Num. 22-36)
		(11) Moses reviews history (Deut. 1-4)
		(12) Law restated (Deut. 5-28)
		(13) Moses' farewell (Deut. 29-34)

THE LAW

The Mosaic Covenant of Law, given during the Exodus, was a temporary set of governing principles which in no way annulled the earlier promises to Abraham. The Covenant promise to Abraham was unconditional, and has the culmination of history in view, for it is then that these promises will be kept. The Law presented conditional promises, stating that obedience would bring to any living generation of Israelites the present experience of blessings God included in the Abrahamic Covenant (see particularly Galatians 3 - 4, and Hebrews 8 - 9).

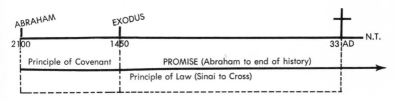

Timeline	Key events	Descriptions
IV. CONQUEST c. 1400 - 1390		
JOSHUA Jericho, Ai (Josh. 6-8)		*Joshua.* Welded into a disciplined and obedient body by God's application of Law, the Israelites under Joshua took the land promised them in the Abrahamic Covenant (Palestine), but occupied only part of it. The book is in two parts: Conquest of the land, 1-12; Division of the land, 13-24. Its theme, demonstrated particularly in chapters 6-8: obedience brings victory and blessing.

Timeline	Key events	Descriptions

V. JUDGES
c. 1390 - 1050

JUDGES
RUTH
1 SAMUEL 1 - 7

Judges. Following the death of the conquering generation, future generations fell into disobedience. Sin led to defeat by surrounding nations and suffering; this to a return to God; God sent a judge to deliver; after a period of rest the people turned away again in disobedience. And the cycle was repeated. As Joshua demonstrates that obedience brings blessing, Judges demonstrates that disobedience brings disaster. The book is organized then: Causes of disaster, 1:1 - 3:6; Cycles of defeat, 3:7 - 16:31; Three portraits of life during the period, 17-21.

Ruth shows that God did not desert the godly few even in times of national decline. A fourth portrait of life during the times of the judges.

1 Samuel 1-7 is a fifth portrait, highlighting the breakdown of the family.

VI. UNITED KINGDOM
c. 1050 - 931

1, 2 SAMUEL
    Davidic Covenant (2 Sam. 6)
1 KINGS 1 - 11
1 CHRONICLES
2 CHRONICLES 1 - 9
PSALMS
PROVERBS
ECCLESIASTES
SONG OF SOLOMON

This period marks the transition from a government by judges to a monarchy. The Israelites were welded into a unified and powerful nation. The basic organization and expansion were under David (author of most Psalms), and consolidation took place under his son Solomon (author of many Proverbs, Ecclesiastes, and Song). This period saw the Jewish people at the height of their prosperity and power.

The books which record the history of the period (1, 2 Samuel, 1 Kings, 1, 2 Chronicles) overlap, as shown in the following chart. Of particular note is the Davidic Covenant: a new revelation that God intends to fulfill His promises to Abraham through a King who will come from David's family line (cf. Luke 1:26-36).

Psalms. This great worship book of the Bible shows the freedom with which we can share every need and emotion with God, the confidence the believer may have in Him, and the wonder of His majesty. The 150 Psalms, short and long poems, range in topic from prophecy to praise, from confession to anger.

Proverbs. This book of practical, pithy insights makes a series of short generalizations about

Timeline	Key events	Descriptions

Timeline / Key events:

Samuel
(1 S. 1-25)

Saul
(1 S. 8-31)

David
(1 S. 16-)

Solomon
(1 K. 3)

1 S A M. (1)
2 S A M U E L (1 C H R O N I C L E S)

1 K I N G S   2 C H R O N
11 · · 9

The historical books dealing with the united kingdom are organized around the lives of these four men.

VIIa. DIVIDED KING-
   DOM — ISRAEL
   931 - 722

1 KINGS 12f   rise of
2 KINGS   the prophets
2 CHRONICLES

   OBADIAH
   JONAH
   AMOS
   HOSEA

Descriptions:

life. It presents the way things *normally* work out, and does not consider exceptions to its rules. While chapters 1 - 7 form a unit in praise of wisdom (defined as "choosing righteousness and rejecting evil ways"), the rest of the book strings together isolated proverbs without organizing them into larger units of thought.

Ecclesiastes. This unique book of the Bible, written by Solomon in a time of personal spiritual decline, specifically sets out to understand life *apart from divine revelation* (see key phrases, "communed with my own heart," 7x; "under the sun," 29x). Its unique value is to demonstrate the despair to which seeking the meaning of life apart from God must drive men. Its organization: Prologue, 1:1-11; Demonstration of the theme, 1:12 - 6:12; Deductions from the theme, 7:13 - 12:8; Epilogue, 12:9-19.

Song of Solomon, taken literally rather than typically or allegorically, portrays the beauty of pure love between man and woman — courtship, marriage, and married love.

After Solomon's death the kingdom split into two parts, Israel (northern) and Judah (southern). Israel was ruled by a succession of evil kings, who to consolidate their power had set up a false worship system in disobedience to the Law. Although warned over and over by prophets like Elijah and Elisha, and the four whose recorded works are in our Bibles (Obadiah, Jonah, Amos, Hosea), Israel persisted in contaminated worship, introducing pagan gods and ways from neighboring countries, until carried into captivity by Sargon II in 722.

The historical books (1, 2 Kings, 2 Chronicles) record the history of the nation and acts of its kings. The moral and spiritual decline is shown there and is sharply portrayed in the prophetic books.

Obadiah. This one-chapter book contains words of judgment spoken against Edom for their enmity to Israel (see the Covenant promise,

Timeline	Key events	Descriptions
ISRAEL 931 Jeroboam		"I will bless those who bless you, and him who curses you I will curse," Gen. 12:3). Causes of Edom's judgment are stated in vss. 10-14.
909 Baasha		*Jonah.* The book records Jonah's call to warn Nineveh, capital of an enemy nation, of God's impending judgment. Jonah, fearing that God might relent if the Ninevites repent (4:2), heads in the opposite direction. Jonah's disciplining, preaching, and the repentance of Nineveh stand as a great affirmation of God's concern for the Gentiles during the Old Testament times, as well as a concrete example for Israel of God's willingness to withhold judgment when men turn to Him.
885 Omri		
OBADIAH		
Elijah Elisha		
841 Jehu		
JONAH		*Amos* is a vivid book of judgment which gives insight into God's concern for social justice, and His anger against the materialistic and complacent. Its major units of thought: Judgment on surrounding nations, 1 - 2; Bases of judgment on Israel, 3 - 4; Call to repent 5:1-17; Nature and inevitability of judgment, 5:18 - 9:10; Final restoration under Covenant promises, 9:11-15.
AMOS HOSEA		
752 last kings		*Hosea* is the touching story of a prophet whose wife's unfaithfulness hurts him, even as Israel's unfaithfulness · has hurt God. Hosea's continuing love culminates in the restoration of a chastized wife, even as God's love is to culminate in the restoration of Israel. Units: The prodigal wife, 1 - 3; The prodigal people, 4 - 14. Note again the restatement of Covenant promises, 13:9 - 14:9.
722 Captivity		

The Prophetic Movement

God had spoken to the people of Israel and Judah through the Law, and clearly warned them of the results of disobedience and sin — as well as encouraged them to righteousness with promises of blessing for obedience (cf. Deut. 28 - 30). When the Covenant people failed to heed the written Word, God sent men to speak for Him. These were the prophets. Normally their message restated truths already known from preceding revelation. At times new information was added within that basic framework. The prophets' messages focused on the moral and religious corruption of their times; announced the judgments God would bring on His rebellious people (and their enemies); and usually extended an offer of reprieve should the people repent. Strikingly, even the most stern of the prophetic pronouncements of judgment consistently include a restatement of the intention of God to fulfill the Abrahamic Covenant. God's purposes remained sure, even though generation after generation of His people rebelled against Him. His Covenant rested unconditionally on His grace and eternal purpose; not conditionally on the works of a given generation.

Timeline	Key events	Descriptions
VIIb: DIVIDED KING- DOM — Judah 931 - 722 1 KINGS 12 - 2 KINGS 2 CHRON.	 Israel de- ported to Assyria	After the division of the kingdom, the south-ern portion, Judah, continued under the rule of the descendants of David. They too de-teriorated, to take part in all the sins of Israel. But Judah did know revival under several godly kings (Asa, Jehoshaphat, Joash). When Israel was destroyed and carried into captivity in 722, Judah survived for nearly 150 years.
JOEL MICAH ISAIAH ┌JUDAH 910 Asa		*Joel* is one of the earliest prophetic writings, earlier than Amos who quotes from it. The theme is divine judgment, growing out of a his-torical plague of locusts which is so terrible that it seems to the prophet to foreshadow that future time when the nation will know God's judgment. The book may be divided: Historic visitation, 1; A prophetic revelation, 2 - 3. Again, the restoration theme concludes the book (3: 17-21).
872 Jehoshaphat 835 Joash JOEL		*Micah* is contemporary to Isaiah, and restates the warning of judgment. Of particular interest is the announcement of individual pardon after national pardon has been rejected by God's re-bellious people. Units: Punishment announced, 1 - 2; Regathering promised, 3 - 5; Individual pardon proclaimed, 6 - 7. Also of note is the strong Messianic note — the deity of the one who is to come from David's royal line is clearly taught, and the fulfillment of the Abra-hamic Covenant promises are to be accom-plished by Him (5:2-15).
ISAIAH MICAH 722 Captivity of Israel		*Isaiah.* This towering book of prophecy is full of new revelations. The large book is divided as follows: Book of judgment, 1 - 35; Historical interlude, 36 - 39; Book of comfort, 40 - 66. Of special beauty and interest in book one are: God's indictment of Judah, 1; The song of the vineyard, 5:1-7; Prophecies of the future, 2: 1-5; 11:1-16. In book two: Portrait of God, 40 - 44; Prophecy of Messiah's death, 53; Por-traits of the time of promise, 60, 65 - 66.
VIII: THE SURVIVING KINGDOM 722 - 586		Judah refused to respond to the warning of judgment that came through prophets and through the destruction of her sister kingdom,

Timeline	Key events	Descriptions

CREATIVE BIBLE STUDY

2 KINGS 18-25 New Covenant Promised (Jer. 30-33)
2 CHRON. 30-36

Israel. The remaining years were ones of increasing darkness, with revivals under Hezekiah and Josiah having only superficial impact on the people. The true state of moral and spiritual life in Judah at the time of the deportation to Babylon is graphically portrayed in Jeremiah 5 - 9, and Ezekiel 7 - 11.

NAHUM
HABAKKUK Judah
ZEPHANIAH deported
JEREMIAH to Babylon

Nahum. The writer's name means "comforter" and his message was one of encouragement to a people who stood in fear of Assyria. The book foretells in striking detail the destruction of its capital, Nineveh. The development: God's goodness and majesty, 1:1 - 2:2; Coming judgment on Nineveh, 2:3 - 3:19.

SURVIVING KINGDOM JUDAH

Zephaniah. From the early, pre-reform days of Josiah's reign, this book shows that God's judgments are approaching Judah and the surrounding nations alike. Outline: Judgments, 1 - 3:7; Final deliverance, 3:8-18. Once again with the announcement of certain judgment comes the assurance of Covenant fulfillment.

722

716 | Hezekiah

Habakkuk. During the Josian reform the prophet is struck by the continuing wickedness of his people. Seeking an answer to why God permits such sin, he is told of God's intention to judge Judah through a national defeat and deportation. Chapters one and two are summarized in this book (chapter 11). Chapter three reveals the prophet's personal struggle for trust as he realizes what the coming judgment will mean to him.

NAHUM

640 | Josiah
ZEPHANIAH
HABAKKUK

JEREMIAH

Jeremiah's life and ministry span the final years of Judah's decline and the series of three deportations of the people from their land (605, 597, 586). Jeremiah spoke to a totally unresponsive people, who opposed and rejected his message, and threatened his life. His message of judgment on Judah was understandably unpopular. Main units of thought are: Indictment of Judah, 2 - 30; Restoration promised, 30 - 33; Judgment on Judah, 34 - 45; Prophecies against the nations, 46 - 51. Of particular note is 30 - 33, which develops further the Abrahamic Covenant promises by foretelling a national conversion associated with their fulfillment: a new heart is to be given to all Israel.

586 final deportation

186

Timeline	Key events	Descriptions

IX. THE BABYLONIAN CAPTIVITY

**LAMENTATIONS
EZEKIEL
DANIEL**

For 70 years Judah's survivors were held in Babylon. During this period the synagogue system was established, the rabbinic (teacher) tradition begun. And during the captivity the people were purged of the tendency toward idolatry, which had caused the falling away from God of past generations.

Lamentations. A poetic work of Jeremiah, expressing the sorrow and anguish of a people torn from the land which, through the Covenant, was so integrally tied to their sense of identity as God's chosen.

Ezekiel, a young man deported with the first group of captives in 605, spoke to the captives at the same time Jeremiah ministered to these remaining in Palestine. Ezekiel's message was the same as Jeremiah's. God is punishing Judah for her sin — deportation is inevitable. Ezekiel has a priestly and temple focus; the present temple of God in Jerusalem is to be destroyed (8 - 11) and a future one to be built on its site at the time of Covenant fulfillment (40 - 48). The main units of thoughts: The prophet's commissioning, 1 - 3; Judgments on Judah, 4 - 24; Judgments on other nations, 25 - 32; Prophecies of restoration, 33 - 39; Prophecies of the restored temple and land, 40 - 48. Of special interest: principles of divine dealing with individuals in a time of national judgment (18), and a detailed outline of events at the end time (34 - 37, 38 - 39).

Daniel is another early captive who rose within the administration of the Babylonian and succeeding empires. The Babylonian captivity marked the last time a king has sat on the Davidic throne. Daniel's prophecy deals with the times during which it was to be unoccupied, the "times of the gentiles." Only Christ remains of the Davidic line, awaiting His return to assume the throne and fulfill the promises to Abraham through a Davidic kingdom. Of particular note in this book is the detailed prophecy in chapter 9, giving the exact date of the appearance of Christ as Messiah in Jerusalem (see *The Coming Prince,* Sir Robert Anderson, Kregel).

THE FRAMEWORK OF REVELATION

Timeline	Key events	Descriptions

X. RETURN TO PALESTINE
EZRA
NEHEMIAH
ESTHER
   HAGGAI
   ZECHARIAH
   NEHEMIAH
		After 70 years, small groups of Jews began to return to Palestine to rebuild the temple and the city of Jerusalem. The first earnest religious motivation soon dulled. By the closing of the Old Testament, we see the people of God living the same life of injustice, disobedience, and insensitivity to God that marked the people before the great judgments of the captivity.

538	1st group returns	*Esther* tells the story of a plot to destroy the Jewish people, and God's providential deliverance through a young Jewish girl.
	temple HAGGAI rebuilt ZECH.	*Ezra* records the history of the early returns, 1 - 6 the return of 538; 7 - 10 conditions at the time of Ezra's return in 458.
	ESTHER	*Nehemiah* picks up the history some years later as this Jewish official in the Persian court returns as governor to rebuild the walls of Jerusalem and to command obedience to God's Law. The moral and spiritual conditions of the time are recorded in Ezra 7:8-10; Neh. 1:1 - 2:8; 10:28-31; 13:4-30.
458	EZRA	
445	NEHEMIAH city walls rebuilt	*Haggai* spoke to motivate renewed work on the temple, which after the foundation was laid had been abandoned for eighteen years. The two-chapter book contains five dated messages, which stimulated the people to finish the temple. Haggai is apparently the only prophet of the Old Testament canon to whom the nation responded!
	MALACHI	*Zechariah* was Haggai's contemporary. His book surveys what Israel can expect during the times of Gentile domination. *Strikingly, this book is filled with the same themes of the pre-exilic prophets!* The returned people have again fallen into disobedience, and an even greater judgment awaits. The Babylonian captivity did not completely fulfill the prophecies of judgment and restoration — it was but a shadow of the end times. The book may be divided: Eight visions of Israel during Gentile times, 1 - 6; Questions of fasting, 7 - 8; Prophecies of the future, 9 - 14. The Messianic emphasis is strong (9 - 10), and the Covenant promises are restated (14).
Closing of the Old Testament history, about 400 B.C.		*Malachi* is the last book of the Old Testament, and demonstrates the corrupting power of sin. Even though purged of idolatry, God's people are rebellious: how desperately the coming

| | | Messiah is needed! The book is organized around a series of seven sarcastic questions the people ask God, and concludes with a promise — and a warning. |

THE NEW TESTAMENT

I. LIFE OF CHRIST ON EARTH
4 B.C. - 33 A.D.

MATTHEW — birth, ministry,
MARK — teaching, death, and
LUKE — resurrection of Jesus
JOHN — Christ

The four gospels give a historical, yet thematic portrayal of the life and ministry of Jesus Christ. Each focuses on His years of public ministry, and contains multiple portraits of Him.

Matthew is written particularly to the Jewish people to demonstrate that Jesus fulfills the Old Testament prophecies about the Messiah. It presents Jesus as the Davidic King, who will return to reign over a people whom He redeemed in His death. Particularly significant to the development of this theme are: Matt. 1 - 2; 16; 24 - 25.

Mark shows Christ as the Man of action, the servant of God involved in His work. Much of the material in Mark is parallel to that in Matthew.

Luke shows Christ as the perfect Man, standing out in stark contrast to the men around Him. His compassion is revealed against their heartless unconcern; His faith against their calculating materialism. Most of the material in 9 - 19 is unique to Luke.

John presents Christ as the Son of God from Heaven. Jesus' Deity is demonstrated in great passages such as John 1, 11, 17, and is clearly taught throughout. Seeing Jesus through John's portrayal, "written that you may believe that Jesus is the Christ, the Son of God, and that believing you may have life in His name" (20:31) has brought many to personal relationship with God.

THE FRAMEWORK OF REVELATION

GROWTH OF THE NEW TESTAMENT

I. Life of Christ	ACTS 1	8	15	21	28
	II. Jewish Church	III. Period of Transition	IV. Gentile Mission	V. Prison Period	VII. Post-Pauline
MATTHEW MARK LUKE	JAMES	GALATIANS	1, 2 THESS. 1 COR 2 COR. ROMANS	PHILEMON EPHESIANS COLOSSIANS PHILIPPIANS	HEBREWS 1 PETER 2 PETER JUDE

189

		VI. Pastoral	1 JOHN
			2 JOHN
		Letters	3 JOHN
		1, 2 TIM.	
		TITUS	

(Period		(Sequence of writing)	
Covered)	33 A.D.	c. 48 - 49	
4 B.C. 33 A.D.			c. 56 - 57
			c. 60 - 62

Timeline	Key events	Descriptions

II. THE JEWISH CHURCH

ACTS 1 - 7   birth of the Church (Acts 2)

JAMES

The Old Testament focus is on the Jewish people, the physical descendants of Abraham and possessors of the Covenant promises. The New Testament focuses on a new and previously unrevealed creation, the Church, called in Scripture the "Body of Christ." Formed after the resurrection of Christ by the Holy Spirit, this company of converted people was to include both Jew and Gentile. The blessings of the promised New Covenant (Jeremiah 30-33), which had been enacted in the death of Christ (Hebrews 8-9) were now made available to all through faith in Him. *Both the Abrahamic and New Covenants have a future fulfillment in view, awaiting only Christ's return to rule our world.* But the blessings to be granted then are offered to present generations. The Old Testament blessings were mediated to the Covenant people through obedience to Law; the New Testament blessings are mediated through responsive faith in Jesus Christ.

The earliest church, however, was an all-Jewish church, as the good news of forgiveness in Christ was preached first in Jerusalem and Judea, as recorded in Acts 1 - 7.

James is the earliest book of the New Testament, written by a leader of the Jerusalem Church to describe that responsive faith which is the key to blessing. James describes the quality of life to which responsive faith will lead.

III. TRANSITION PERIOD

ACTS 8 - 15   the Jerusalem Council (Acts 15)

When Gentiles responded to the gospel message of forgiveness and personal relationship with God in Christ, the Jewish Church was amazed. Brought up in the Old Testament framework of thinking, with its clear distinction between Covenant people and all Gentiles, the church struggled to understand what God was

190

Timeline	Key events	Descriptions

GALATIANS

doing now. Acts 8 - 15 records the struggle of the church with this new and unexpected aspect of God's eternal purpose.

Galatians may have been written later, but definitely deals with the theology of the transition. In it Paul discusses in detail the relationship between Law and Faith; both as alternate avenues to salvation and as keys to different life-styles. Its units: Paul's ministry, 1:1 - 2:10; Legalism's limitations, 2:11 - 4:8; Legalism's bondage, 4:8 - 5:15; The principle of faith, 5:16 - 6:10. This is the key book for anyone trying to understand God's way of life for believers today.

IV. GENTILE MISSION

ACTS 16 - 21   The first missionaries (Acts 15: 36f)

With the Church now composed of both Jew and Gentile, it entered into a period of aggressive missionary work. The apostle Paul, more than any other, was responsible for carrying the Gospel to the known world, linked together by a common language (Greek) and common government (Roman). Acts 16 - 21 records Paul's missionary travels and covers the period during which the following letters were written.

1 THESSALONIANS
2 THESSALONIANS
1 CORINTHIANS
2 CORINTHIANS
ROMANS

1, 2 Thessalonians are possibly the first of Paul's letters written to believers in a city he visited only briefly. Reference to many major doctrines shows how thoroughly he taught new converts the basics of the faith. Particularly see Paul's description of his missions strategy (1 Thess. 1 - 2) and many references to God's plan for the future (1 Thess. 4; 2 Thess. 2).

1 Corinthians was written to answer questions raised by the church at Corinth. It deals with divisions in the church (1 - 4); church discipline (5 - 6); marriage (7); personal rights that conflict with other's consciences (8 - 10); church customs (11); the exercise of spiritual gifts (12 - 14); the resurrection (15). Perhaps best known is Paul's discourse on love (13).

2 Corinthians is an intensely personal letter in which Paul expresses his understanding of the ministry, and shares his feelings and experiences. Particularly important is 8 - 9, which develops principles of giving for the age of faith which are distinctly different from the tithe of the Old Testament.

Timeline	Key events	Descriptions

Romans. The basic theological book of the New Testament, Romans carefully examines the nature and impact of the salvation won on Christ's cross. It discusses: Imputed righteousness, 1 - 5; Experienced righteousness, 6 - 8. Paul then goes on to show in 9 - 11 that God has not abandoned His Old Testament plan for His Covenant people, but that an unrevealed interlude (the Church age) has been interjected. The book concludes (12 - 15) with a study of the life to be lived in and by the Church.

V. PRISON EPISTLES

ACTS 21 - 28

PHILEMON
EPHESIANS
COLOSSIANS
PHILIPPIANS

Paul's success in evangelism brought him into conflict with the Roman government, for its policy permitted only "licit" religions. During imprisonment he wrote several letters which are included in our Scriptures.

Philemon is a short, one-chapter letter to a believer appealing to him to welcome back as a brother a runaway slave Paul had won to Christ while in prison.

Ephesians gives a distinctive picture of the Church as a single, functioning Body. Shown are the origin of the Church in God's eternal purpose (1), past and present status of believers (2), the quality and power for transformed lives (3 - 4), and practical expression of the new life in Christ (5 - 6). Of special interest are two prayers: 1:16-23; 3:14-19.

Colossians focuses on who Christ is and what relationship with Christ means to believers. Written to counteract a philosophy which viewed religious faith as unrelated to life in the world, Paul shows Christ's involvement as Creator, Incarnate, and sufferer of bodily death. The believer's spiritual life in Christ is to be lived *in the world.* Units: Theological argument, 1 - 2; Practical application, 3 - 4.

Philippians. This short, personal letter centers on the theme of joy. Even in prison Paul finds cause to rejoice — and reveals sources of joy for believers that are independent of circumstance.

VI. PASTORAL LETTERS

1 TIMOTHY
2 TIMOTHY

Three letters to young ministers are included in our New Testament:

1 Timothy portrays believers as members of a single family, and discusses relationships within

Timeline	Key events	Descriptions
TITUS		the church. Units: Charge to Timothy, 1; Behavior in the church, 2 - 3:15; Guidelines for leadership, 3:16 - 6:2; False teachers, 6:3-18.

2 Timothy portrays the Christian life as a warfare demanding dedication. Units: God's call, 1; The believer's duty, 2:15-26; The enemy's strategy, 3 - 4:5; Future reward, 4:6-18.

Titus builds on the theme of godliness, setting high standards for Christian life. It shows that godliness is possible only because of God's transforming grace provided in Christ.

VII. GENERAL EPISTLES

HEBREWS
1 PETER
2 PETER
JUDE
1 JOHN
2 JOHN
3 JOHN

Other New Testament books, not written by Paul, are called the General Epistles. These were likely written after the apostle's death, directed to various groups.

Hebrews. Written to Jewish-Christian communities, this letter presents the superiority of Christ to the life-style of the Old Testament. Key words: "better than." The main line of argument compares Christ's Person (1 - 4) to angels and Moses, and His work to the Old Testament priesthood (4 - 8:6), Mosaic Covenant (8:7 - 9:14) and sacrifice (9:15 - 10:18). Chapter 11 discusses faith; 12, God's disciplining of His children apart from Law.
    Other features are a series of four warnings inserted in the main line of argument: 2:1-14; 3:7 - 4:13; 5:11 - 6:12; 10:19-39).

1 Peter. Outlines the pattern of life for believers facing persecution. See outline, p. 143.

2 Peter, Jude. In 2 Timothy 3 Paul warns against a coming apostasy (falling away). Both these books explore this topic in detail, exposing the methods, motives, and activities of counterfeit Christians. 2 Peter 3 is a prophetic picture of the fate reserved for this world after God's revealed (Old and New Testament) purposes are accomplished.

1 John is developed around the theme of fellowship with God. It shows how believers can be sure they are living in fellowship with Christ. Units: Provision for fellowship, 1:5 - 2:2; Proofs of fellowship, 2:3-29; Love and the new nature, 3:1 - 4:21; Fellowship and faith, 5:1-21.

THE FRAMEWORK OF REVELATION

193

Timeline	Key events	Descriptions
		2, 3 *John* are short, one-chapter personal notes to individuals.
	VIII. PROPHECY REVELATION	*Revelation.* This last book of the Bible presents a view of future events which integrates Old and New Testament prophecy. Jesus Christ is to return as Messiah, the Savior-King of Israel and Lord of lords over the whole earth after accomplishment of the judgments against which the O.T. prophets warned. Units: John's vision, 1: 1-19; Letters to contemporary churches, 2 - 3; Climax of history, 4 - 22. Because the book echoes and integrates the entire O.T. prophetic outlook, use of a commentary in working through it is recommended. The best probably is John Walvoord's *The Revelation of Jesus Christ* (Moody Press).

Principles

Section 1.

Seek to live Scripture, not just learn about it.

Section 2.

LIFE AT ISSUE: to go from life's concerns to find God's guidance in Scripture . . .

10. Define a shared *concern.*
11. Search for *several* relevant Scripture *passages.*
12. Let the *biblical perspective* shape your *response.*

BUILDING UNDERSTANDING: to start from Scripture to seek God's perspective on life . . .

13. Gain an overview of *developed thought.*
14. *Follow thought* closely by *paraphrasing.*
15. *Generalize* to *specific personal applications.*

Section 3.

RESOURCES: to develop a grasp of broader principles of Bible study . . .

16. Locate passages in their *Scripture framework.*
17. Scripture is one Book; a unit, woven from many.
18. *Define* personal experiences as *concerns.*

18
Typical Concerns

Life for all of us falls quickly into familiar
patterns: patterns that become habits.
But every now and then something happens
that jolts us from our comfortable and
familiar ways of life. We're forced to
make new decisions, to respond to something unexpected. Or perhaps something
we read makes us wonder about a
pattern in our life.

It's at times like these we need to define
our experiences — into concerns.

There it was when Carl walked into the drive-in grocery! Right on the counter, where the kids from the nearby high-school — and everyone else — couldn't miss seeing it. A whole stack of those magazines, with naked and near naked girls seductively posturing on the cover.

Upset, Carl grabbed the carton of milk he'd come into the store for, picked up an evening paper and paid the woman, wife of the middle-aged man who'd just taken over the franchise. Looking rather grim, uncertain about what to say or how to say it, Carl simply hurried out the door.

    ❊   ❊   ❊   ❊   ❊   ❊   ❊   ❊

Exhausted, Mary slumped in her favorite chair beside the FM radio. She reached back to massage her neck: one of those horrible headaches was beginning. She felt its familiar probing; knew how easily it would become a pounding up toward the top of her head.

How many times had she and Amy argued this week? That girl! At sixteen she knew everything — and how she resented rules. Or even advice. "But she's young. So immature. She's *got* to listen. . . ."

It was so hard to know how to communicate. Even to know when a parent should set rules. Or the kinds of rules. Kids had to learn to make decisions for themselves sometime.

Not everyone should be parents, Mary thought wryly. *Not*

195

people like me. She reached over and turned on the FM, then leaned back, rotating her head rhythmically, hoping the headache would go away.

❂ ❂ ❂ ❂ ❂ ❂ ❂ ❂

Life Stays With Us

Sometimes headaches do go away. But life doesn't. Life stays with us, and brings with it the unexpected situation — or the all-too-common one — that leaves us disturbed and shaken. How are we to respond to them? How do we handle uncertainty, doubt? The easy way is to try to avoid painful experiences, or to struggle to ignore them. Carl simply won't go into that store again. Mary, who has to live with her problem, will turn to soothing classics on FM in an attempt to forget the recurring arguments with her daughter, and dull the physical pain they cause.

Run away from it?

Ignore it?

We can try, of course. But life with all its realities rushes in on us again and again — and reminds us that, as Christians, we're called to live Christ's life *in* the world. In this world. This world of sin, of stress, of injustice, of pain, and of the unexpected experience that leaves us uncertain and confused.

Somehow the Christian can't afford to treat the painful as an occasion for retreat. To the Christian, each fresh experience is an invitation from God to learn more of Him, and to live more of Him.

The Bible is God's unique resource, given to help us transform uncertainty to opportunity and tragedy to triumph. Experiences like Carl's and Mary's are often given us by God to stimulate our growth; to lead us to Scripture and fresh discovery of reality as God knows it and as He wants us to express it in our lives. Rather than withdrawing from life's jolting experiences, we need to see them for what they are: God's invitations. Invitations we need to accept if we're to grow to maturity.

Invitation Accepted

How do we accept the invitations that God extends to each of us through the experiences of life? Basically, by defining our experiences as a concern, and bringing our concern to God, to search out His help in the Scriptures.

Defining experiences. Experiences like Carl's and Mary's normally flood us with feelings. It's these feelings, feelings of frustration and futility, that we try to reduce by flight. Usually we're so busy trying to get away from them that we resist thinking about the experience that caused them. It was an unpleasant experience — too painful to dwell on.

But if we're to handle our feelings effectively, we need to face them. By coming to understand situations that give rise to such feelings, we can learn to respond positively, to reduce frustrations by creatively expressing God's will through our lives.

It's necessary, then, to relive painful experiences. I don't mean the way we often relive them — simply rerunning them to berate ourselves for supposed or real failures. I mean to relive them *in search of understanding.* To rethink the experience, to ask "why" of our feelings, to pose the kind of questions that will help us pierce to the core issues which the experience has raised.

Take a look again at Carl's experience. It's easy to see why he was upset and concerned. The moral deterioration of our society is all too obvious; the flaunting of sin as "personal freedom" and a "right" of the "mature adult" is all too common a hypocrisy. But there were other things that had added to Carl's jolting shock. He'd never seen that kind of magazine in the drive-in before. In fact, the last couple to run it, now returned to the laundry business in Denver, had chatted with him of their determination to keep the store a "family" one. Then, too, Carl felt some responsibility for his community, and for the high school (attended by his own son) just two blocks from the store. Still, he didn't feel free to infringe on the rights of the owners. He couldn't *demand* they remove the magazines. Or picket the store, or do any of the other things people do today to try to force their ideas and ways of life on others. And then, too, he wondered about a chance to witness to the new owners. He'd known the old ones well — even given them a couple of Christian books. Would his witness be helped or hurt if he said something about the magazines? Was it better to ignore them, with the intention of trying to become a friend first, and perhaps winning the owners to Christ?

All these thoughts flickered through Carl's consciousness, and, uncertain about the answers, blocked by his uncertainty from any positive action, Carl felt frustration — and ran. And the feeling of futility created by that frustrated retreat made the experience too painful to think about later.

But later is just the time to think about it. Later, when there's no pressure for immediate decision to frustrate us. Later, when there's time to sort out the issues and, with our questions defined, to search the Scripture for guidance.

As concerns. If Carl had thought over his experience as we just have, and isolated some of the questions on which he needed God's viewpoint before he could work out his response to the new situation, his experience would have jelled into a *concern.* By a "concern" I mean a *formulated question about reality which can direct our search in Scripture for God's guidance in life.*

From Carl's experience at least two *concerns* arise: How am I as a Christian to relate to non-Christians? How am I as a Christian to respond to sin in my society?

We could follow the same process in Mary's experience with her daughter Amy. The swirl of questions about guidance, communication, rules, etc., that have overwhelmed her and so many others in our day may also be expressed as concerns: How am I as a parent to live with and guide my children?

In fact, *all our experiences,* as we grapple with them in search of understanding, can be defined as concerns. And this definition can lead us into fruitful, purposeful Bible study.

God's answer. It's important to understand the kind of answer we'll find when we bring our concerns to God's Word. We won't find rules. Carl won't find lists of five do's and two don'ts. Mary won't find a list of "three steps to successful parenthood for mothers of girls like Amy."

What we will find is God's portrait of reality. We will find the world exposed to us as it really is; the basic principles on which life operates and on which interpersonal relationships operate. When we grasp the reality, we'll understand any specific directions God may give, and have insights into His way to respond in situations where there are no specific directions, Scriptural guidelines.

Actually, the idea that there are situations for which we can find no specific rule shouldn't surprise us. Life is complex; cultures differ. No one experiences life just the way we do, faces the same complex of circumstances. And even for an individual, circumstances and situations change. We can't treat every person the same way. Sometimes, because timing differs, the right response at one time may be the wrong one at another. Because situations and persons do differ, God doesn't often give detailed rules: do's and don'ts for "every occasion." Oh yes, there are some. "Don't commit adultery" is one. *That* doesn't vary with situations. "Don't lie," the Bible says. And there aren't any exceptions suggested.

But in most situations, situations like those faced by Carl and Mary, *the response each will make will be situation-specific.* It will be an individual response to *these* people in that *store* (not for all people in every store, or for every believer).

But if most of our responses to life are situation-specific, does Bible study really help? And if so, *how* does it help?

I've suggested earlier in this book that the Bible is an objective, "out there" portrait of reality. It is accurate and trustworthy. *Understanding reality* as God has shared His perceptions of it with us provides the *necessary framework for making decisions as Christians. Any response we make in a situation is to be in harmony with the biblical portrait of reality, and the way of life suitable to it.* The Bible, then, is essential to us as an objective standard against which to check our responses to life.

But the Bible is more than God's objective tool of guidance. The Bible is His *personalized* means of guidance as well.

Scripture makes it clear that every Christian has as his constant companion the Holy Spirit of God, who settles into his life and personality with the initial decision to trust Christ as Savior. What it all means is simply this: *the Person who wrote the Bible is with us to interpret it to us.* When we discover in Scripture the objective guidance for living it provides, the Holy Spirit is with us to lead us in applying

199

that guidance to specific situations.

This great truth is reflected by James when he says, "If any of you lacks wisdom, let him ask God, who gives to all men generously and without reproaching, and it will be given him" (James 1:5). Wisdom, the ability to apply truth to specific decisions in life, is ours from God for the asking. When we have grasped the principles of the Word, we can trust God to guide our application of them to our lives.

And this, I believe, is what John means when He speaks of the Holy Spirit who rests His touch on our personalities and says, "and you have no need that any one should teach you" (I John 2:27). Our life with God is to be one of responsiveness *to Him*. No one can live our life for us; no one can play God over us. We can, of course, learn from others — others with whom we study the Bible, our pastors who help us understand its meaning. But ultimately, the Holy Spirit must be our Teacher.

And we must, each one, be His student.

Coming to know God's Word, led to deeper knowledge by experiences that we define as Christian concerns, and guided by His provision of objective truth and personalized application, we face life confidently — and with trust.

Typical Concerns

Chapter 12 of this book suggests several avenues of approach to Scripture to discover God's viewpoint on our concerns. The following list of typical concerns — a short and suggestive list, to be sure — includes a few of the passages to which a basic knowledge of Scripture might lead one, some of the Bible characters who may have shared experiences like those giving rise to the concern, and some key words for concordance study. This is "starter" help only, and is not an exhaustive or complete listing. It's given to help you launch a group study or, should any of these be your concerns, for personal study. And it's given that with this kind of starter help you might develop Bible study skills.

❋　❋　❋　❋　❋　❋　❋　❋

1. How am I as a Christian to relate to non-Christians?

Passages	Parallel	Key words
Matt. 6:43f	*experiences*	witness
Luke 10:25f		testimony
1 Cor. 5:9f	Daniel	light
Titus 3	Joseph	
1 Peter 2 - 4	Paul (Acts)	

2. How am I as a Christian to respond to sin in my society?

Passages	Parallel	Key words
Matt. 5:13f	*experiences*	world
Eph. 5:1-13		justice
Ps. 1, 15	Amos	righteousness
Isa. 5:1-23	Nehemiah	judge/judgment

3. Does our personality really go on living after death?

Passages	Parallel	Key words
1 Cor. 15	*experiences*	life/living
Luke 16:19-31		death
John 20	Jesus	resurrection
2 Cor. 5:1f	resurrection	eternal
1 Thess. 4	appearances	
Rev. 20 - 22		

4. What can I count on the Holy Spirit for?

Passages	Parallel	Key words
John 14 - 16	*experiences*	Spirit
Gal. 5:13-35	Paul, in	strengthen/ed
Rom. 8	2 Cor.	
Eph. 3:14 - 4:2		
1 Cor. 12		

5. Does praying do any good?

Passages	Parallel	Key words
Matt. 6:9-13	*experiences*	hear/answer
Luke 11:1-13		prayer
James 5:13-20	Daniel	supplication
John 17	Elijah	thanksgiving

6. What should my attitude toward money and material things be?

Passages	Parallel	Key words
Mal. 3:6-18	*experiences*	trust
Ps. 49		riches
Luke 12:13-34	rich fool	wealthy
Matt. 6:19-34	rich young ruler	
2 Cor. 8, 9	Solomon	

7. How am I as a parent to live with and guide my children?

Passages	Parallel	Key words
Deut. 6:1-9	*experiences*	instruct
Ps. 128		discipline
Prov. 31	Israel like	chastise
Titus 2	children,	children/child
Heb. 12	Exod. 14 - 19	father

8. How am I to live with others in Christ's Church?

Passages	Key words
Matt. 18:15-35	one another
John 17	brethren/brother
Rom. 12 - 15	love
1 Cor. 12 - 14	unity
Ephesians	body

9. What's so special about me? Am I really important?

Passages	Parallel	Key words
Matt. 10:26f	*experiences*	gifts
Luke 13:31f		compassion
Luke 15	Moses,	servant/son
	Isaiah	unworthy

10. What's God's attitude toward me when I fail Him?

Passages	Parallel	Key words
Ps. 32, 51	*experiences*	forgiveness
Ezek. 18		restoration
Hosea 11	Peter's denial	propitiation
Micah 7:7-20	Jonah	sin
1 John 1:5 - 2:2		steadfast love

Use of Tools

Principles

Section 1.

Seek to live Scripture, not just learn about it.

Section 2.

LIFE AT ISSUE: to go from life's concerns to find God's
guidance in Scripture . . .

10. Define a shared *concern*.
11. Search for *several* relevant Scripture *passages*.
12. Let the *biblical perspective* shape your *response*.

BUILDING UNDERSTANDING: to start from Scripture to seek
God's perspective on life . . .

13. Gain an overview of *developed thought*.
14. *Follow thought* closely by *paraphrasing*.
15. *Generalize* to *specific personal applications*.

Section 3.

RESOURCES: to develop a grasp of broader principles of
Bible study . . .

16. Locate passages in their *Scripture framework*.
17. Scripture is one Book; a unit, woven from many.
18. *Define* personal experiences as *concerns*.
19. *Subordinate all tools* to the biblical *text*.

19
Use of Tools

I once knew a pastor who got up every
morning at 6 A.M. to study. I was terribly
impressed when I heard it; for I knew
him as a fine and very busy man. But
I wondered. If he studies so faithfully,
why are his sermons so superficial?
Then I learned what it was he studied.
Not the Bible itself, but commentaries on
the Bible. And I understood.

Sometimes it seems hard to get it straight. "The *Word of God* is living and active . . ." (Heb. 4:12). Or in Christ's words, "Sanctify them through the truth, thy Word is truth" (John 17:17).

Not the commentary.

Not men's words about the Word, but God's Word itself: living, active, powerful, transforming.

That's why in creative Bible study we want to keep books about the Bible carefully subordinate to the biblical text. And the books that have highest value as resources should be those that help us make our own discoveries in Scripture. What kind of books are available to the Christian layman? How should they be used? Which should have highest priority on our "to buy" list? In this chapter we'll look briefly at three types of books, and comment on their usefulness.

Discovery Aids

The Christian layman who comes to Scripture for God's guidance in life will want several tools to help him discover God's viewpoint.

1. *Concordance.* A good concordance which lists each occurrence of every word in the Bible is essential. As discussed in chapter 3, the best concordance is an exhaustive one which enables you to trace each word of the English text back to its Greek or Hebrew original. *Strong's Ex-*

haustive *Concordance* and *Young's Analytical Concordance* are examples of this type. Those students who have a limited knowledge of biblical Greek and Hebrew vocabulary will find *The Englishman's Greek Concordance of the New Testament* and *The Englishman's Hebrew and Chaldee Concordance of the Old Testament* helpful. *Cruden's Complete Concordance* is the best known concordance on the English Bible (King James Version).

2. *Versions and translations.* In searching for the meaning of Scripture passages it is helpful to compare various translations of the biblical text. Actual translations attempt to reproduce the original Greek and Hebrew texts as closely as possible without interpretation; paraphrases, on the other hand, openly attempt to restate meaning interpretatively in contemporary English idiom. The use of both translations and paraphrases is recommended but one should work primarily in one basic, accepted translation or version — using the other translations and paraphrases for reference.

Among the more familiar translations and/or versions are:

King James Version. Translated 400 years ago; many meanings are obscured by archaic language.

American Standard Version. An updating of the King James Version, published in 1901 and recently revised as the *New American Standard Bible.*

Revised Standard Version. A good modern translation which, although unacceptable to some, has established itself as the most widely used contemporary version of the English Bible.

New English Bible. A recent British translation.

Modern Language Bible — The New Berkeley Version in Modern English. Widely used by American evangelicals.

Those paraphrases most familiar include:

Phillips New Testament in Modern English. An excellent paraphrase by J. B. Phillips, one of the first of the moderns and in some ways still the best.

Taylor's *Living Bible.* Kenneth N. Taylor's recently completed paraphrase of the entire Bible which often captures brilliantly the argument of passages. Not so good in the Old Testament.

Good News for Modern Man. The American Bible

Society's widely acclaimed "loose" translation of the New Testament. Not without its faults.

Amplified Bible. An amplification of the biblical text attempting to show shades of meaning in most verses by the use of several renderings of key words in the verse.

There are many other translations and versions available which are helpful for comparison and added insights.

Background Aids

Many customs of Bible times are reflected in the biblical text but are strange to the twentieth century Christian. Often the political and economic setting of a period is reflected in a particular book of the Bible and the teaching of that book becomes clearer when the historical background is understood. A variety of reference works are available to provide this background information — making the biblical world more understandable and highlighting the biblical writer's meaning by his use of certain words, phrases, situations, illustrations, etc., which otherwise might be missed. The Bible student will want to add several volumes from the following categories to his library of background aids:

1. *Bible handbooks.* These inexpensive and information-filled reference books attempt to provide background information of all sorts on the Bible and its world, and some of them even give a concise comment on the entire text of the Bible. A good Bible handbook is probably the first background book a layman should purchase. Popular books in this category include: H. H. Halley's *Halley's Bible Handbook,* M. F. Unger's *Unger's Bible Handbook, and* D. E. Demaray's *Bible Study Sourcebook.*

2. *Bible surveys.* Surveys of the Old and New Testaments attempt to place the text in its historical setting and normally include outlines and analyses of the individual books of the Bible. *The Old Testament Speaks* by S. J. Schultz, *New Testament Survey* by M. C. Tenney, and *A Survey of the New Testament* by R. H. Gundry are recommended.

3. *Bible histories.* Books on Bible history relate biblical events and books to the broader context of the times. Unlike surveys, they do not include outlines and analyses of the individual biblical books. A history provides an

excellent source of supplementary material when a Bible book has been located in the framework of God's developing revelation (see chapter 8). Good reference works in this category include A. Edersheim's *Bible History — Old Testament,* M. C. Tenney's *New Testament Times* and L. J. Wood's *Survey of Israel's History.*

4. *Biblical archaeologies.* Old and New Testament archaeology books relate the discoveries of archaeologists to the Scriptures, often adding fascinating insights into customs and life style in Bible times. Such works also provide evidence for the authenticity and accuracy of the biblical text. Non-professional students of the Bible will find the following books helpful: *Archaeology and Bible History* by J. P. Free, *Archaeology and the Old Testament* and *Archaeology and the New Testament* by M. F. Unger, and *The Archaeology of the New Testament* by E. M. Blaiklock. One should also consult books on Bible manners and customs.

5. *Bible dictionaries.* These reference tools include brief articles on places, persons, and things in the Bible. The articles discuss both the familiar and unfamiliar — from "pharisee" and "publican" to "Urim and Thummin." Bible dictionaries are usually one volume works whereas Bible encyclopedias (an expanded dictionary) are frequently published in several volumes. Since a distinctive theological viewpoint is reflected in most works of this sort it is suggested that you obtain one that is published by an evangelical publisher. Recommended dictionaries which, for the most part, contain up-to-date material include: *The International Standard Bible Encyclopedia* (an older work), *The New Bible Dictionary* and the *Zondervan Pictorial Bible Dictionary.*

6. *Bible atlases.* A Bible atlas focuses attention on the lands of the Bible, showing by map and illustration the significance of geographical-historical settings in the development of Scripture. *Baker's Bible Atlas, The Wycliffe Historical Geography of Bible Lands,* and *The Zondervan Pictorial Bible Atlas* will be found useful.

Interpretation Aids

Books in the preceding areas are aids to personal discovery. They *help you understand* what *you* read in Scripture. Books in the following area — interpretation aids — characteristically *tell you* what others believe the Scripture

208

CREATIVE BIBLE STUDY

means or teaches. To me, this seriously limits their value. We need to come to the Word to hear God's voice — not a man's voice telling us what God says. Reading books in this category should never become a substitute for a study of Scripture itself, and should never be used as a shortcut to understanding the meaning of Scripture.

These books then, when they are used, should be used *after* a person has come to a tentative interpretation of Scripture through his personal search and discovery — and then only to check for pro or con arguments which may have been overlooked. Only after a personal study of the Word are we in a position to evaluate the opinions of others.

A list of interpretation aids might include:

1. *Commentaries.* There are various types: one volume commentaries on the whole Bible or New Testament; multi-volume commentaries on the Bible; commentaries on single books of Scripture. The latter are of greatest value because they normally include extended discussion of the background of a book and carefully try to follow its main theme. The single-volume commentary on the Bible or New Testament is of less value although some are helpful in determining the meaning of the text.

2. *Word studies.* This type of work is frequently beneficial for it adds many fresh insights from the original languages. The disadvantage of this type of book is psychological: too often one comes to depend on the author's study of Scripture rather than going to Scripture to seek meaning and application for oneself.

3. *Topical treatises.* There are many books on biblical and doctrinal topics which seek to present the teaching of Scripture on a particular subject. These are often helpful, but again they must be kept subordinate to one's personal study of the biblical text. This demands that we seek to develop our own understanding from the Word first — before turning to the thoughts of men.

Certainly the thoughts of others who have given their lives to the exploration of God's Word have much to add to our own understandings. But we are only able to evaluate the opinions of others when we have a personal grasp of Scripture. Developing our own understanding of the Word deserves priority over all other reading.

To summarize then, there are books which ought to be in the library of the Christian layman as aids to personal Bible study — books which will help us explore, interpret, and apply God's Word. A *basic library,* one in reach of and of value to laymen as tools for personal Bible study would include:

1. Three or four versions of Scripture — two translations, two paraphrases.
2. An exhaustive concordance.
3. A Bible handbook.
4. A good Bible dictionary.
5. A reliable Bible atlas.

Appendix:

Two Paraphrases

Paraphrase of James 2:14-26

What's this big deal about the kinda guy who spouts, "I got faith," but doesn't show it? You know *that* kind of faith doesn't save anyone, don't you?

Look at it this way. Here's a couple that's really in rags. They don't know where their next meal's coming from. And this joker piously smiles, "Well, good luck. Hope you get some food and clothes." It's pretty plain his good wishes don't mean a thing! It's just that way with faith. The kind of faith that only exists as good intentions, man, that's dead. Real faith works.

In fact, someone is sure to say to the dead faith-er, "So you got faith? I got actions. You prove your faith to me without actions — if you can. But I'll let my actions show my faith." And he'd have the guy cold.

And don't come back with, "I agree with God. I believe He's One." Big deal. Even the demons believe that — and it scares them to death!

You have to be shown that faith isn't just nodding your head when someone reads a Bible verse? Look at Abraham. Wasn't his claim to faith proven by his actions? Why, "he offered up his son Isaac upon the altar." You see? "Faith" and "actions" are a team. They always pull together in a fella's life. They're two sides of the same coin, and you have to mint the "action" side to complete "faith" and make the whole thing genuine. Actually, Abraham's action only fulfilled the Scripture that says, "Abraham believed God, and it was reckoned to him as righteousness." It proved God was right when He said, "Abraham believes . . ."

❂ ❂ ❂ ❂ ❂ ❂ ❂ ❂

So we have to face it. Separate body and spirit and you've got a corpse. Separate faith and the action that flows from it and you've got the same thing. Just dead faith. And dead faith doesn't mean, beans, fellas. Not beans.

Paraphrase of I Peter 3:19-22

For Christ once even *died* on account of sins, the righteous dying instead of the unrighteous, in order that He might bring us again to God, His body being put to death, His spirit bringing Him to life again. By the same Spirit He also preached to the spirits now in prison, who were once disobedient and disbelieving (this occurring when the patience of God eagerly waited the repentance of men in the days when Noah was constructing the ark in which few, that is eight persons, were brought safely through the waters of judgment). And now *you* are saved by something that corresponds to this picture of deliverance, i.e., baptism's making you a member of Christ, which points in essence not to getting rid of the filth of the flesh through His death, but points to the appeal of a cleansed conscience to God which is yours through His resurrection.

Scripture Index

INDEX

NOTES

NOTES

NOTES

NOTES

NOTES

NOTES

NOTES

NOTES

NOTES